Buses mean business

STAGECOACH

AND ITS SUBSIDIARIES

VOLUME TWO

Keith A. Jenkinson

An Autobus Review Publication

First published August 1991
Reprinted March 1992

ISBN 0 907834 24 8

Stagecoach has standardised on the Alexander-
bodied long wheelbase Leyland Olympian for all its
new double deckers and these are now represented
in almost all its English fleets. Typifying these is
G702TCD which was originally placed in service
with Southdown Portsmouth with whom it is seen
here opposite Southsea's South Parade Pier on
22 April 1990.   (Ian Buck)

Autobus Review Publications Ltd.,
42 Coniston Avenue, Queensbury,
Bradford, West Yorkshire BD13 2JD.

FOREWORD

Since the publication of volume 1 of the company's history, Stagecoach has grown to be the largest independent bus company in Europe and can now be described as a multi-national concern. This rapid growth has been the result of much hard work, innovation and enthusiasm on the part of our management and work force and it has been exciting to be a part of this team.

We hope that you will find the continuation of our story of interest.

Brian Souter

Ann H Gloag

INTRODUCTION

Despite being only just over ten years of age, Stagecoach has grown from a small acorn planted in 1980 into a strong and mighty oak. From its humble beginnings, it has developed into an international concern controlling several major bus companies in Britain as well as spreading itself into Africa, Aisa and North America.

When volume 1 of Stagecoach's history was published in the autumn of 1988, it was never dreamed that the expansion of the company would be so great that a second volume would be required so quickly. The complexity of many of the events of the last three years have in some instances been difficult to unravel and I am extremely grateful to the company's management team for assisting me in several areas, and answering my numerous questions. In particular, I extend my thanks to Brian Souter, Ann Gloag, Derek Scott, George Watson, Brian Cox and Neil Renilson for reading through the draft text and adding much additional detail to the book and to Isabel Peters for her help in several

directions, not least her endless patience on the occasions that I have needed to telephone her. I must also record my thanks to Peter Lutman and Rod Bailey for their assistance in respect of Stagecoach Malawi's operations and also to the many photographers whose work has greatly enhanced this publication, and in particular to Ian Buck, Andrew Izatt, Murdoch Currie, Campbell Morrison, Brian Pritchard and Thomas W.W.Knowles who have provided the views which would otherwise have proved elusive.

I hope that those reading this book will gain as much pleasure as I have gained in writing it, and who knows, perhaps a third volume will be necessary in the not too distant future in order to progress the intriguing story of Stagecoach's ongoing development.

K.A.Jenkinson.
Queensbury, Bradford.
June 1991

3

Although Fife Scottish has been included in the list of Stagecoach Group companies and fleet names shown opposite, at the time of writing although Stagecoach Holdings Ltd. had been named as preferred bidder for this SBG subsidiary, its sale had not been concluded.

STAGECOACH
MAGICBUS
PERTH PANTHER
INVERNESS TRACTION

BLUEBIRD NORTHERN

FIFE SCOTTISH
BUZZBUS

CUMBERLAND
KIRKPATRICKS
COACHLINE
CMS CARLISLEBUS

RIBBLE
ZIPPY

EAST MIDLAND
MANSFIELD & DISTRICT
MAUN MINIBUSES
MIDLAND TRAVEL (COACHSTYLE)

UNITED COUNTIES
STREET SHUTTLE
CORBY'S MAGIC MINIS
ROUTEMASTER
COACHLINKS

HASTINGS & DISTRICT
HASTINGS BUSES
HASTINGS COACHES

SOUTHDOWN
CEDARBUS
COASTLINE
EASTBOURNE & DISTRICT

HAMPSHIRE BUS
STAGECOACH

STAGECOACH MALAWI

GRAY COACH LINES

SPEEDYBUS ENTERPRISES
必 達 巴 士 企 業 有 限 公 司

Front cover :

One of a number of Leyland Nationals acquired from Stagecoach's English subsidiaries during the summer of 1989 for use at the start of the Perth 'bus war', 219 (VKE568S), an ex,East Midland example which began life with Maidstone & District, travels along Kinnoull Street in the heart of the city enroute to North Muirton on service A in August 1989.. Proudly sporting Perth Panther fleet names, it also has a route diagram painted above its side windows.   (S.K.Jenkinson)

Back cover :

left column, top to bottom :

Showing the colourful livery used by Maun of Mansfield upon the takeover of the company by East Midland, ex.Kelvin Scottish Alexander-bodied Leyland Leopard TSU642W is seen here in 1989. (P.T.Stokes)

United Counties Plaxton Paramount-bodied Leyland Tiger 121 in Stagecoach corporate livery with Coachlinks fleet names arrives at Victoria Coach Station, London on the X50 service.   (Travelscene)

Still wearing Portsmouth Citybus livery despite now being owned by Southdown Portsmouth, Alexander-bodied Atlantean 326 heads towards Southsea on 3 March 1990 closely followed by sister bus 323 which sports a different style fleet name. (Ian Buck)

Wearing the attractive Bluebird livery of Northern Scottish, MacDuff-based Duple-bodied Leyland Leopard NPE44M rests in Aberdeen bus station in the spring of 1990.   (Travelscene)

Right column, top to bottom :

Carrying a small Southdown fleet name vinyl below its windscreens, Top Line Leyland National 22 (BCD822L) shows the revised livery used by the company (which omits the black skirt) as it passes through Hastings on 6 March 1990.   (Ian Buck)

One of Stagecoach Malawi's former Kowloon Motor Bus Co. Daimler CVG6s, 1018 was painted in an all-over advertising livery and is seen here in service in Blantyre in November 1989.   (R.Bailey)

Hastings & District low-height Bristol VRT 559, still wearing its pre-Stagecoach livery arrives in its home town on 6 March 1990. New to Maidstone & District in 1979, it passed to the Hastings fleet upon its formation in 1983.   (Ian Buck)

Illustrating Ribble's red & grey livery. Leyland National 738 leaves Preston bus station at the start of its journey to Bolton on the 126 service in the autumn of 1989.   (K.A.Jenkinson)

THE CONTINUING STORY OF STAGECOACH

Taking up the story of Stagecoach and its subsidiaries from where it was left in Volume 1 in October 1988, it will be remembered that at that time the company was a mere eight years of age. Having first entered the passenger transport industry in March 1980 with a secondhand Ford Transit minibus, Stagecoach grew in stature year by year, expanding first in its native Scotland and then moving south of the border in April 1987 with the purchase of Hampshire Bus and Pilgrim Coaches from the National Bus Company. Although some 480 miles from its home base, this sharpened the company's appetite to gain further expansion in England and before the year had ended, NBC subsidiaries Cumberland Motor Services Ltd. and United Counties Omnibus Co. Ltd. had been acquired to give Stagecoach a firm foothold upon which to build in the years ahead. During the next twelve months, the group's corporate identity became firmly established as vehicles from all its newly-acquired companies were being transformed into their striking new standard livery of white with red, blue and orange stripes and chevrons which, in addition to presenting a unified image, allowed them to be transferred more easily between its subsidiaries whenever this was deemed necessary.

Looking at each of the subsidiaries during the autumn of 1988 finds a scene which was continually changing with buses being reshuffled between them with some rapidity. United Counties had, on the penultimate day of August, surprisingly purchased a pair of V-registered Plaxton-bodied Ford R1114 coaches from Northamptonshire independent, Yorks of Cogenhoe, these bringing this make of chassis back into the fleet after a considerable absence. No sooner had these arrived than United Counties acquired a trio of Robin Hood-bodied Iveco 49.10 minibuses which were diverted from Hampshire Bus for whom they had been originally intended. On 18 September these were joined by the other three minibuses of this batch which were received from Hampshire Bus in exchange for three Alexander-bodied Mercedes L709D buses. Prior to this, United Counties had despatched their seven little Carlyle-bodied Ford Transits - inherited earlier from Hampshire Bus - to Carlton PSV Sales of Hellaby who immediately placed them in service in their subsidiary SUT fleet for operation in Sheffield. Having now disposed of more minibuses than they had acquired, United Counties then found it necessary to hire a Robin Hood-bodied Iveco 49.10 from Luton & District on 1 September and after a period on loan, this was eventually purchased by the company on 4 October.

The first of the series 3 Bristol VRTs bought from Devon General began to arrive in the early autumn and were divided between United Counties and Hampshire Bus where they

Illustrating the old-style Hampshire Bus fleet name and Stagecoach-group corporate livery is Bristol VRT 433 (FDV834V), one of a number of buses of this type acquired from Devon General. (F.W. York)

were to be joined by further buses of this type during the months ahead. Also making their debut at Northampton during October were two of the three ex.Southdown NCME-bodied Leyland PD3s which, since their acquisition by the Stagecoach Group in August, had reclined at Keswick bus station. These were to be used as driver training vehicles by their new owner and it was not intended that they should be used in a passenger carrying role.

Meanwhile, Hampshire Bus had in August withdrawn from service the last five examples of its once large fleet of ECW-bodied Bristol LH6L single deckers and, as has already been chronicled, exchanged a number of its minibuses with United Counties.

Up in Cumberland, following Brownriggs (Cook & Marshall) of Egremont's withdrawal from stage carriage operation on 21 September, Cumberland Motor Services purchased that company's five surplus minibuses and two coaches. The latter, a Leyland Leopard and a Bedford YMT, both of which carried Plaxton bodies, were not used by their new owner and were instead placed in store until their eventual sale in

Repainted in Stagecoach-group corporate livery, Cumberland's ex.Brownriggs MCW Metrorider 91 (E855BRM) leaves Workington bus station on town service 48 in April 1989. (A.Gilmour)

November. Also withdrawn from service at this same time were five of the Bedford coaches and a Ford Transit minibus acquired by Cumberland earlier in the year with the Kirkpatrick business, these being replaced by a number of ex.United Counties Leopard coaches and two of the more recent ex.Brownriggs coach-seated minis - an Iveco 49.10 and an MCW Metrorider, all of which were immediately repainted into Kirkpatrick's colours. The other Iveco 49.10 (with Robin Hood bus bodywork) obtained from Brownriggs was despatched on loan to Hampshire Bus towards the end of September together with Cumberland's ex.Kirkpatrick Ford Transit. Instead of returning to their rightful owner, both vehicles were moved from Hampshire Bus to United Counties on 18 November for a continuing period of loan.

The arrival of the new Alexander-bodied Leyland Olympians allowed Cumberland to withdraw their remaining nine ex.Hampshire Bus former London Transport Daimler Fleetlines, all of which immedietely found a new home with the expanding Merseyside independent, Fareway of Kirkby. Before entering service, the new 87-seat Olympians were all fitted with fare boxes for use on Carlisle's busy city services. Also leaving Cumbria in the early autumn were the two Plaxton-bodied Volvo coaches which had been on loan from

Still wearing NBC poppy red livery, albeit with Carlislebus fleet name, Cumberland's former Hampshire Bus/London Transport Daimler Fleetline 1923 (OJD169R) overtakes one of Cumberland's ex.Kelvin Scottish Routemasters, 907 (WLT824), in Carlisle city centre. (K.A.Jenkinson)

Replacing Cumberland's ex.Hampshire Bus Fleetlines were a number of new Alexander-bodied Leyland Olympians, one of which (1006) is seen in Carlisle city centre before receiving its fleet names. (A.Gilmour)

Stagecoach, Perth since 26 July. One returned home towards the end of September while its sister gave another couple of weeks service before being despatched north of the border.

Still experiencing a shortage of minibuses, Hampshire Bus hired a Carlyle-bodied Ford Transit from Alder Valley South during September, retaining this until the following month when it was able to be returned to its rightful owner. Four of the company's seven Ford Transits hired by United Counties to Carlton PSV came home in November, the remaining three staying in Sheffield with SUT for whom they were eventually purchased by their masters, carlton PSV Sales.

Stagecoach's activities had by now spread overseas and were no longer confined to Scotland and England. During a visit to Hong Kong by Brian Souter and Ann Gloag in the spring of 1988, the purpose of which was to view the operations of the renowned Kowloon Motor Bus Company, contact was made with Clement Lau Ming-Chuen, an engineer who had on 27 June 1986 formed a company under the title of Speedybus Services Ltd. to supply former Kowloon Motor Bus Company buses to the Peoples' Republic of China. Seeing an opportunity to become involved in bus operation in this part of the world, Stagecoach International Services Ltd. struck a deal with Mr.Lau which, on 15 November 1988 resulted in the birth of Speedybus

Enterprises Ltd, a company in which Stagecoach International and Speedybus Services each held a 50% share. As Kowloon Motor Bus Co. had at that time a large number of withdrawn double deckers for which there appeared to be no resale market, Speedybus Enterprises purchased a number of these half-cab Metsec-bodied Daimler CVG6s and some former London Daimler Fleetlines with a view to operating them in the Peoples' Republic of China in a similar fashion to those already despatched by Speedybus Services. Following contact with a Hong Kong-based advertising agency, agreement was reached to paint these buses in all-over advertising liveries and supply them free of charge for operation in several Chinese cities on three-year contracts in return for the rental income from the advertisers. Although the buses retained their right hand driving position, they had their entrance doors altered from the nearside to the offside and as will be seen later, their success was such that by the start of 1991 no fewer than 42 buses (20 CVG6s and 22 Fleetlines) had been thus crossed the border via Speedybus Enterprises in addition to 10 CVG6s and 16 Fleetlines supplied to China by Speedybus Services.

The early autumn months crept along quietly north of the border with both Stagecoach and Magicbus experiencing little change to either their operations or fleets and it was not until November that this period of stability was broken. During that month, Stagecoach began a massive clearout of their surplus vehicles, a process which was to continue into December and almost clear the company's Spittalfield premises of the large quantity of vehicles which had built up over the previous twelve months. This clearout was not unconnected with the fact that the vehicles were parked on land not owned by Stagecoach and the owner's reaction subsequent to the discovery of a large quantity of buses on their land concentrated Stagecoach's mind on the need or otherwise of actually accommodating elsewhere what could at best be described as 'scrap' vehicles. Many of the ex. Kelvin Leopards which, since their purchase in the autumn of 1987, had slowly donated parts to others of their type in the Stagecoach fleet were sold to the Lanarkshire breaker, Dunsmore of Larkhall and whilst some were doomed to disappear beneath the breaker's torch, a small number managed to escape by finding new owners with whom they continue their role as spare parts providers. In addition, three of the former Kelvin Leopards which had operated for Stagecoach in an all-white livery were taken out of service and sold for further use - one to Scarlet Band of West Cornforth, Co.Durham and two to Galston Motors, Barvas - while the six Leopards which had been stored at Keswick bus station since their return from Hampshire Bus were all sold to Moffatt & Williamson of Gauldry. Also included in the clear-out were all but one of the Magicbus / Cumberland / Hampshire Bus ex. South Yorkshire PTE Van Hool McArdle-bodied Volvo Ailsa double deckers. Of these, seven were sold for continued PSV service (3 to Safeway, Dagenham and 4 to Blue Triangle of Liverpool) whilst the others stayed closer to home, one being sold for use as a playbus in Fife, the other, a heavily cannibalised example which had never been operated by the Stagecoach group, passing to Irvine of Law for spares.

To replace the three all-white liveried Leopards taken out of service and sold in November, a trio of the ex.Kelvin buses of this same type which had been purchased a year earlier were taken out of store at Spittalfield and, after receiving an unrelieved white livery, made their debut in a revenue-earning capacity on 1 December.

The field adjacent to Stagecoach's Spittalfield depot provided home to a large number of withdrawn and reserve buses in May 1988 including Bristol Lodekkas, ex.Kelvin Leopards and a Bristol MW. (K.A.Jenkinson)

Having greatly reduced the number of surplus vehicles which had been gathererd in the field alongside the former McLennan depot at Spittalfield, those still remaining were transferred to new positions behind and between the nissen huts which constituted the depot itself, thus removing the 'Elephants' Graveyard' from the field which was in any event not owner by Stagecoach, much to its owner's pleasure ! In addition, a small area of land opposite the depot was sold for the purpose of building a house. A similar tidying up operation was also conducted at Stagecoach's Walnut Grove premises in Perth and following the removal of the two recently-acquired ex.McIntyre LD6G Lodekkas to Spittalfield for cannibalisation in September, the wartime Bristol K5G which had been bought for possible preservation was resold to the Eastern National Preservation Society and returned to its native Essex in November.

By now, rumours had begun to circulate that Stagecoach was planning to go to the Stock Market and become public in the not too distant future in order to raise the necessary additional capital following an expression of interest in the Scottish Bus Group when this was privatised. These rumours were however, quickly and strongly denied by Stagecoach who pointed out that having already purchased three English companies in the NBC privatisation programme without going public, why should they do so now ?

Prior to this, Stagecoach had experimentally introduced the Bristol VRT to their Scottish fleet with the hire of a solitary example from Cumberland Motor Services. Still wearing NBC poppy red livery and complete with Cumberland fleet names, it was used on several services including that from Pitlochry to Aberfeldy and although not known at that time, was to herald a great influx of this type of vehicle north of the border during the following couple of years.

Seeking to improve their prestigious Glasgow and Edinburgh to London services which had been acquired in October 1987 following the collapse of the Cotters empire, Stagecoach introduced a new two-tier service on 7 November on which passengers could choose between standard or super service. Four of the company's Neoplan Skyliners (C719JTL and E91-3VWA) were converted for this new operation, the 'super service' being applied to the exclusive 'luxury' 14-seat lower deck which was fully partitioned, upholstered and carpeted and in which no smoking was permitted. As part of the 'super service', passengers were given free newspapers and magazines. At this same time, the 'standard service' was also enhanced by the removal of 6 seats from the upper deck to improve leg room and all journeys were given a faster overall time between termini. Free tea and coffee was offered on all standard and super class journeys and sandwiches, pastries, snacks and cold drinks could be purchased from the hostess onboard. In London, the terminal point was altered from Kings Cross to Victoria Coach Station in order to provide better facilities and Stagecoach proudly claimed that not even British Airways could match their new service. Whilst standard fares were the same as those previously charged by Stagecoach between Scotland and London, the 'super service' fares although of course higher than those charged to 'standard' passengers, were actually slightly cheaper than those on the former Cotters 'Coachline' operation. Also introduced at this same time was a new 'Weekender' service from London to Glasgow, Edinburgh, Cumbernauld, Livingston, Dunfermline, Stirling, Perth and Dundee with timings which were more convenient for weekend trips. One such departure for instance left London at 2.30pm and reached all its Scottish destinations before midnight.

No sooner had Stagecoach's new Anglo-Scottish operations got underway than it was announced by Bruce of Airdrie that they were to start a new daily service between Airdrie, Coatbridge, Glasgow, Hamilton and London Kings Cross at the end of November, operating this under the title 'Londonliner'. Far from pleased by this intrusion, Stagecoach immediately made plans to retaliate by the introduction of an identical service operated by Magicbus. For this purpose,

One of the last Neoplan Skyliners to be purchased new by Stagecoach, E92VWA is seen here lettered for the company's 'Super Stagecoach' anglo-scottish service from London to Aberdeen a few days before its sale to Tayside Travel Services in August 1989. (Ian Buck)

Painted in an all-white livery with Magicbus fleet names for use on the service from Glasgow to London in competition with Bruce of Airdrie, Duple-bodied DAF C895CSN rests in Buchanan bus station, Glasgow in July 1989. (K.A.Jenkinson)

Stagecoach's four Duple-bodied DAF coaches (C892--5CSN) were transferred to Glasgow and were repainted into an all-white livery with 'Magicbus Londonlink' predominantly added in red lettering to each side and across the rear.

As a result of the reorganisation of its London services, Stagecoach divested itself of five of its ex.Cotters Van Hool-bodied Volvo B10M coaches which were transferred from their Glasgow base to Cumberland Motor Services during October and November. The remaining two examples of this type were reallocated to Perth for continued operation by Stagecoach who, prior to this, on 5 December had lost the tender for, and thus relinquished, their Blairgowrie town service and stage carriage route from Blairgowrie to Kirriemuir to another local independent, Meffan of Kirriemuir.

Stagecoach's English subsidiaries continued to make changes to their fleets, and as a result of the arrival of more series 3 Bristol VRTs from Devon General, both Hampshire Bus and United Counties were able to withdraw a number of their older buses of this type. Several Leyland Nationals were also taken out of service by these two companies and following a revision to their minibus operations, Hampshire Bus were able to withdraw four of their Ford Transits and six Dormobile-bodied Freight Rover Sherpas, the Fords being quickly sold to Transit Holdings.

Having made a start on renumbering their fleet by the subtraction of '3000' from the original fleet number, Hampshire Bus completed this task in December whilst United Counties who, for many a long year had favoured cast metal fleet number plates, the base colour of which denoted the depot to which the vehicle was allocated, discontinued this practice in favour of conventional fleet number transfers. A novel feature applied to all United Counties' new Alexander-bodied Leyland Olympians was the fitting of special glass to the small intermediate side windows on both decks. When viewed from the outside, the opaque windows carried advertising on a blue background for the company's local services, whilst from the inside the windows appeared transparent and thus allowed passengers a normal, unimpeded view.

The flow of series 3 Bristol VRTs from Devon General continued with a further eight arriving in December, these being divided equally between Hampshire Bus and United Counties. Cumberland meanwhile loaned two of their surplus minibuses - an Iveco and a Ford Transit - to United Counties who then hired the Iveco to London Buses for short term use at Catford. One of Cumberland's ECW coach-bodied Leyland Leopards also departed for two weeks loan to Stagecoach at Perth during December, although this returned home before 1988 ended.

Surprisingly, no further businesses had been purchased since May and the second half of the year had been a period of consolidation rather than expansion. During November, a management reorganisation had taken place during which Barry Hinkley, the managing director of Cumberland Motor Services, additionally took over this position at United Counties. In the following month, Ewan Brown, a Scottish Transport Group board member and director of merchant bank Noble Grossart who in January 1988 had resigned his position with STG was appointed to the board of Stagecoach, thus bringing more expertise to the company.

As if to highlight what was to come during 1989, at the start of the new year Stagecoach announced that they had gained the backing of seven major Scottish financial institutions - Murray Ventures plc; TSB Scotland plc; Noble Grossart Investments Ltd.; The Standard Life Assurance Co.; Scottish Development Agency; Scottish Investment Trust plc and Scottish Eastern Investment Trust plc - who had underwritten the issue of £5million-worth of new equity capital. This was the first time that Stagecoach had approached the financial institutions for funding of such a nature and whilst plans had

Two of United Counties long wheelbase Alexander-bodied Leyland Olympians, 633 and 628 stand side by side in Biggleswade's tiny bus station in the town's square on 3 May 1989. (K.A.Jenkinson)

been laid for massive expansion during 1989, it was stated that it was unlikely that the company would be seeking further equity capital in the foreseeable future. Following the assurance of this financial backing, Stagecoach held exploratory talks with Strathclyde Regional Council in the hope that they might be able to purchase the council-owned Strathclyde's Buses operation, but this was not to be progressed further at that time as the undertaking's privatisation plans 'went cold'. It was not until February 1991 that Strathclyde reopened its privatisation file and started taking any real action towards a move into the private sector. Letters were also sent to most of the 50 municipal and regional operators in local authority ownership and as a result several meetings were arranged in an attempt to gain further expansion for the Perth-based company.

The first Leyland National to be operated in Scotland by Stagecoach was ex.Hampshire Bus GFX974N which was acquired in January 1989. When painted in corporate livery three months later, it was given unusually narrow horizontal stripes, these being altered to conventional dimensions at a later date. Seen at Walnut Grove depot, Perth, fresh from the paint shops on 31 March 1989, it was the following day returned to Glasgow for continued use in the Magicbus fleet. (K.A.Jenkinson)

Pressed into service immdeiately upon its arrival from Devon General, Stagecoach Bristol VRT FDV833V still in NBC poppy red livery, approaches Stanley on an early evening journey to Blair Atholl on service 22 on 31 March 1989. (K.A.Jenkinson)

Following the evaluation of the Cumberland Bristol VRT north of the border, it was permanently added to Stagecoach's Scottish fleet at the start of January when it was joined by four buses of this same type acquired from Devon General. These were immediately placed in service in Glasgow and on Tayside still wearing their former owner's NBC poppy red and white livery, although their repainting into Stagecoach corporate colours quickly commenced later in that same month. Another stranger to cross the border at around this same time was a 41-seat Leyland National which, still sporting Hampshire Bus livery, entered service in the Glasgow-based Magicbus fleet on 18 January. Evaluated on services 22 (Castlemilk to Bridgeton) and 67 (Glasgow to Lennoxtown),‟it was used for several weeks before being despatched to Spittalfield where it received the group's corporate colours. Also purchased by Stagecoach during January was a Plaxton Paramount 4000-bodied Neoplan which had received fire damage whilst in service with its previous owner, Amberline of Liverpool. Wearing National Express Rapide livery, this was acquired solely for spares and was parked behind Walnut Grove, Perth depot for gradual cannibalisation. On the debit side, the three Routemasters - former London WLT703 and 847DYE and ex.Northern General FPT598C - which had been extensively

Purchased by Stagecoach for spares in January 1989, fire-damaged National Express Rapide liveried ex.Amberline of Liverpool Plaxton 4000-bodied Neoplan C177KHG is seen in a state of cannibalisation at Walnut Grove depot, Perth some two months later. (S.K.Jenkinson)

cannibalised at the Spittalfield graveyard, were completely dismantled on site by Lanarkshire breaker, Dunsmore of Larkhall.

Following a short period of calm, Cumberland once again became involved in a bus war which attracted attention from Cumbria County Council officers. This took place in Maryport where Richard Smith had started a town service during May 1987. Unlike Cumberland's town service, Smith's penetrated the town centre and offered a revised route to the Ewanrigg Estate, the route being timed to slot into Cumberland's half hour frequency to offer a combined 15-minute service. The major operator then stepped up the frequency to three buses per hour and subsequently to four and abandoned their original route to follow that used by Smith, timing their journeys two minutes ahead. This resulted in vehicles of both operators battling for passengers and often stopping side by side when picking up, thus causing unnecessary congestion particularly in the town centre. Although no action was taken by the County Council, they were nevertheless unhappy about this situation which continued until June when Smith finally conceded defeat and withdrew his service.

HIGHWAYMAN CAPTURED

On 1 February, George Watson, formerly managing director of Clydeside Scottish, at that time the Scottish Bus Group's most progressive subsidiary company, joined the Stagecoach Group and was immediately seconded to Harry Blundred's Transit Holdings to advise on the setting up of Transit's Docklands scheme in London. Nearer home, Stagecoach acquired the operations and vehicles of Highwayman Coaches of Errol, just a few miles from their Perth headquarters. As was chronicled in volume 1 of the Stagecoach history, Highwayman had been formed by Robin Gloag upon his departure from Stagecoach in 1983 and although having embarked upon stage carriage operations for a short time, had been mainly involved in contract and coaching activities, developing a series of excursions in addition to undertaking occasional Scottish Citylink work. Although Highwayman's five vehicles - 3 Volvo B58s including the first of this type to be purchased by Stagecoach, a Neoplan Jetliner and a Whittaker-bodied 23-seat Mercedes L608D minicoach - and a shoppers service for Tesco Stores were included in the deal, Highwayman's depot at The Hideout, Errol was retained by Robin Gloag from where he was to concentrate on bodywork repairs and spraying. As part of the agreement reached, Stagecoach guaranteed an initial one year contract for repainting and some body repair work, and although Robin Gloag was also hopeful of additionally gaining a number of outside contracts, he was optimistic that longer term contracts might eventually be negotiated with the Stagecoach Group.

Initially, the acquired ex.Highwayman vehicles were operated by Stagecoach still sporting their former owners colours and fleet names, but were eventually transformed into corporate colours as part of the ongoing standardisation programme. Withdrawn by Stagecoach were four Alexander-bodied Leyland Leopards, one of which had been damaged in an accident, and two of Magicbus's ex.London Routemasters. One of the latter was placed in Stagecoach's reserve fleet for possible future re-use whilst the other had suffered severe roof damage in a low bridge accident in Glasgow and was unlikely to be repaired. One of the company's Duple Dominant III-bodied Volvo coaches was downgraded from its London duties by having its toilet removed and its seating increased from 50 to 57.

United Counties, having added a further 7 ex.Devon General Bristol VRTs to its fleet in January, gained another 4 from this source in February and sold 10 older buses of this type to Ensign (dealers) of Purfleet. Before these left their

Still in full Highwayman livery some weeks after its acquisition by Stagecoach, Neoplan Jetliner B169BFE leaves Walnut Grove depot, Perth on 31 March 1989 to take up a private hire duty. (K.A.Jenkinson)

original owner, several exchanged their moquette-covered seats for those fitted to UCOC's younger VRTs which were covered in PVC, although their bench seats could not be exchanged due to their incompatibility. Also added to the United Counties fleet, albeit only temporarily, was a Robin Hood-bodied Iveco 49.10 minibus which was hired from Luton & District for driver training purposes. Another stranger in this area was a South Wales Transport Leyland National 2 which was fitted with numerous DiPTAC features and was touring the country to enable operators to gain first hand experience of these modifications. Arriving at United Counties in February, it remained with the company for four weeks during which time it was used on a variety of services. The battle to woo more passengers from the increasing number of taxis in Corby continued at pace and with the use of United Counties Routemasters, the company felt that it was gradually winning the battle. From February 13, several evening industrial journeys were merged with Corby's town service in order to improve facilities whilst the company gained several Leicestershire school contracts - one of which made use of Uppingham outstation's solitary Bristol VR - and an Asda 'free bus' service.

Still resplendent in Highwayman livery, Whittaker-bodied Mercedes 608D minibus A121XWB prepares to leave Stagecoach's depot at Walnut Grove, Perth on 21 August 1989, several months after the acquisition of the Highwayman business. (K.A.Jenkinson)

During its demonstration to operators around Britain including some Stagecoach subsidiaries, South Wales Leyland National 829 which incorporated a number of DiPTAC features spent a period of time in service with United Counties. Given temporary fleet number 13 by UCOC, it is seen here in Bedford on 9 March 1989 whilst in use on local service 102. (T.G.W.Carter)

New to Cumberland Motor Services, Reeve Burgess-bodied Dodge S56 minibus D22SAO was transferred to Hampshire Bus during 1989 and is seen here in corporate livery at Basingstoke bus station in August of that same year. (Ian Buck)

ORY640, one of the ex.Cotters of Glasgow Van Hool-bodied Volvo B10M coaches acquired by Stagecoach was towards the end of 1988 transferred to Cumberland Motor Services. Looking immaculate in Cumberland's white & red Coachline livery, it arrives at Southport on a private hire duty on 14 June 1989. (K.A.Jenkinson)

As part of a drive to improve travelling conditions, Hampshire Bus banned smoking on all its stage carriage vehicles and became the first of Stagecoach's subsidiaries to make such a move. On 10 February, Hampshire Bus also gained the tender for operation of the 202 service from Petersfield to Alton, a route previously maintained by Alder Valley. On the vehicle front, another Bristol VRT arrived from Devon General in January and a further 3 in February while Plaxton Paramount-bodied Volvo coach 142 was reregistered from 5142SC to A613TCR, its 'SC' number being returned to Stagecoach at Perth for use on a Neoplan Skyliner.

During February, Cumberland Motor Services took delivery of their much-publicised three-axle Leyland Olympians. Fitted with Alexander bodywork, these two double deckers were equipped with coach-type seating for 96 passengers. Used on a variety of duties including the Sellafield works contract and the Border Clipper service to Carlisle, their massive dimensions created few problems and they quickly gained favour with both passengers and crews alike. Having received a new white & red Coachline livery, Cumberland's ex.Stagecoach Van Hool-bodied Volvo coaches had their seating increased from 40 to 48, this being achieved by the removal of the toilet compartment and although the company permanently transferred three of its Reeve Burgess-bodied Dodge S56 minibuses to Hampshire Bus, it surprisingly received an Alexander-bodied Mercedes 709D mini from the latter source.

An even greater surprise was the purchase for Hampshire Bus of three new Duple bus-bodied 63-seat Dennis Javelins which it was stated were for evaluation purposes. Arriving on

3 March, all three were placed in service from Winchester depot a couple of weeks later and quickly settled down alongside that town's Leyland Nationals with few teething troubles. On the 5th of March, Hampshire Bus opened a new outstation in the yard of Short Brothers (builders) at Botley, mainly to provide vehicles for use on the 33 service from Hedge End to Winchester via Botley and on 2 April reopened their former outstation at Bedford Road lorry park, Petersfield for the recently acquired 202 route.

Hampshire Bus further increased its minibus fleet during April when two new 25-seat Robin Hood-bodied Iveco 49.10s were purchased and three more Reeve Burgess-bodied Dodge S56s were acquired from Cumberland in exchange for a trio of Alexander-bodied Mercedes 709Ds. Added to these was a three-axle Talbot Pullman which was borrowed by Hampshire Bus from its manufacturer on 24 April for a three month evaluation.

During this time, United Counties also gained four new Robin Hood-bodied Iveco 49.10s and additionally hired a Ford Transit from Hampshire Bus. Also borrowed from the Department of Transport during March was a Berks & Bucks Bristol VRT which had been modified to incorporate a number of DiPTAC features whilst Plaxton-bodied Leyland Tiger coach 83 was re-registered from 83CBD to A294ANH, its cherished number being transferred to 105 (NBD105Y), another Leyland-Plaxton. At this same time, 83 was repainted into National Express's new 'London Express' livery.

In Scotland, two of the ex.London Routemasters withdrawn from service during the early months of 1988 were gradually

1201, one of Cumberland's two coach-seated Alexander-bodied three-axle Leyland Olympians shelters in the shade at Lowther Park, near Penrith in June 1990 whilst undertaking a private hire duty. (K.A.Jenkinson)

being cannibalised for spares at Magicbus's Warroch Street depot, Glasgow while another bus of this type - 628DYE was withdrawn early in March following accident damage whilst on service. This was removed to Spittalfield whilst its future was decided and soon afterwards this too was used as a source of spares. The remaining Volvo Ailsa which had remained in store at Spittalfield following the sale of its sisters was finally broken up for scrap during March.

Following the success of Magicbus's Londonlink service which had operated at weekends in competition with Bruce of Airdrie since January, it was decided in March to extend this to operate nightly. With a fare which undercut Bruce's £10 single and £18 return and Stagecoach's own 'standard' £13 single and £23 return, the new nightly operation immediately attracted good loadings and often required the operation of duplicates.

EXPANSION AT HOME & OVERSEAS

After a long period of comparative calm during which much consolidation had been achieved, Stagecoach surprisingly purchased United Transport International's 51% stake in Malawi's national transport company in Central Africa on 31 March 1989, the remaining 49% of which continued to be held by the Malawi Government. With its headquarters in Blantyre, United Transport Malawi Ltd. operated a fleet of 258 single deck buses and coaches, the majority of which were Leyland Victory Mk.1 and Mk.2 models fitted with locally-built bodywork. These maintained a wide range of urban and inter-urban routes throughout the country and the company was operationally divided into three regions - Southern, Central and Northern. Founded in 1947 as the Nyasaland Transport Company and operating only one route (from Blantyre to Zomba with locally-assembled Bedford OB buses), the company grew to become Malawi's largest bus and coach operator and at one time also operated a fleet of heavy lorries for general haulage work. In 1964, following

Malawi's independence, Nyasaland Transport, which was by that time operating 108 buses throughout the country, was renamed United Transport (Malawi) Ltd. and in 1970, following amicable discussions with the Government, the company relinquished its exclusive right as the sole operator

of bus services in Malawi, and a number of local independent operators then began to emerge. In 1982, all the remaining freight vehicles were disposed of to leave United Transport free to concentrate on their passenger-carrying activities.

Following their sortie overseas, Stagecoach Holdings once again turned their attention to further expansion in England and on 7 April purchased East Midland Motor Services Ltd. together with its subsidiaries Frontrunner (SE) Ltd., Frontrunner (NW) Ltd. and its 50% stake in East Midlands Transport Advertising. Only days before its acquisition by

Stagecoach, East Midland had purchased a share in Forrest of Mansfield - a removal and storage company - and also acquired Rainworth Travel of Langwith, an independent bus and coach operator. This added more than 300 buses and coaches to the combined Stagecoach fleet and in addition launched the Scottish company into new territories including the north-east fringe of London.

East Midland was a typical former NBC company whose fleet was made up largely of Leyland National single deckers, Bristol VRT and Leyland Olympian double deckers and Leyland Leopard and Tiger coaches. Also operated were a tiny handful of Bristol LH6L buses and a few MCW Metrorider and Mercedes 608D minibuses together with oddments of other types. Although the company's main operating area was in north Nottinghamshire and Derbyshire where depots were located at Worksop, Retford, Mansfield, Chesterfield, Shirebrook and Clowne, upon deregulation East Midland had established a new base in Essex where they had gained several contracted services, operating these first under their own name and later under the newly-adopted title of Frontrunner South East from premises at Wyatts Green, Debden and Rainham. Similarly, East Midland ventured into the Greater Manchester area from a new base at Tintwhistle near Glossop, eventually placing this under the new Frontrunner North West banner. In order to provide the additional vehicles needed for their two remote Frontrunner operations, a number of secondhand Leyland Atlanteans were acquired from Greater Manchester PTE and Grampian Regional Transport as well as more secondhand Leyland

Nationals and Bristol VRTs. Using a corporate livery of two-tone green and cream, East Midland's vehicles were given fleet names appropriate to their operating company - i.e. East Midland, Mansfield & District, Frontrunner North West, or Frontrunner South East.

Although almost all of the then present management of the company remained in place after the takeover by Stagecoach, George Watson who had recently returned from his secondment to Transit Holdings was appointed as managing director of East Midland and took up his new duties immediately. Within hours of taking control, three Leyland Nationals were hired to Frontrunner South East by United Counties, remaining in Essex from 8 April to the penultimate day of that month. More unusually however, East Midland received a Routemaster on loan from United Counties and acquired three further buses of this type from Magicbus. Although the United Counties example was immediately used in service for evaluation purposes, the latter trio were placed in store to await a decision on their future use. The early appearance of Routemasters in the east midlands was not at all surprising in view of George Watson's enthusiasm for this type of bus, as in addition to owning a preserved example himself, it was he who had introduced them to Clydeside Scottish in 1985 and had, along with Brian Cox, been instrumental in starting the 'provincial Routemaster revival' of the mid / late 1980s which led around twenty operators buying and running this type of bus during the period 1985 - 1990. East Midland's services quickly came under scrutiny by its new masters and almost immediately several changes were implemented in order to provide improved and more profitable operations. Amongst these was the replacement of the X1 and X3 express services, operated jointly with Trent Motor Traction, by a new service numbered X1 running hourly between Sheffield and Nottingham. Marketed under the title of 'Steel Arrow Express', this was operated solely by East Midland who used a trio of Leyland Tiger coaches on this new operation. The

X67 service from Mansfield to Liverpool via the Peak District and Manchester which had previously run only on three days each week became daily and continued to be maintained jointly with Hulleys of Baslow whilst a series of circular tours to the picturesque Peak District from towns in Derbyshire and Nottinghamshire on Sundays, Bank Holidays and Wednesdays during school holidays was launched and were available without the necessity to pre-book.

Not all the news was being made south of the border however, for in Scotland Magicbus had received a new three-axle Alexander-bodied Leyland Olympian which took the honour of being Britain's largest bus - a legend proudly proclaimed in large letters on each side of its body. Christened the Megadekka, it had seating for 110 passengers and following much publicity, it entered service on 10 April. Surprisingly, it was used largely on school contracts in the Glasgow area where it replaced two vehicles, although it did regularly work evening peak journeys on Magicbus' normal stage carriage service to Easterhouse. Also acquired was yet another Bristol Lodekka, this being a rear entrance FS-type which had been delivered new to Lincolnshire Road Car Co.Ltd, and owned latterly by preservationists. Despite being allocated a fleet number, it was not placed in service and instead was parked behind Spittalfield depot where it soon began to be used as a source of spares. Also joining the Scottish fleet was another former Hampshire Bus Leyland National whilst the 'original' bus of

this type was, after a period in store at Walnut Grove, Perth, returned to service with Magicbus, Glasgow in full corporate livery - albeit without fleet names. This surprisingly replaced a Routemaster which was then despatched to Spittalfield to join the reserve fleet. Returning 'home' at the beginning of March was A613TCR, a Plaxton-bodied Volvo coach which had started life with Stagecoach registered A799TGG, was later re-registered 5142SC and was transferred to Hampshire Bus in July 1988. Meanwhile, Stagecoach discontinued the former Highwayman service between Perth and Errol from 2 April, covering this with existing services, and announced this change by affixing hand-written paper notices to the windows of several of its single deck vehicles.

No sooner had the dust settled on the East Midland acquisition than it was announced that Stagecoach Holdings had, on 21 April, purchased the operations and vehicles of Ribble Motor Services of Preston from its management. Ribble's extensive property portfolio was not all however included in the deal, some of this remaining with Dimples Estates Ltd., the company owned by three of the original team who bought Ribble from the NBC in 1988 and two property developers, although Stagecoach were to lease those properties necessary to the company's operations. With a massive fleet of some 838 vehicles, Ribble's acquisition when added to Cumberland Motor Services gave Stagecoach an operating area stretching down the western side of England from the Scottish border to Manchester and included the former United Transport International minibus networks in Preston and around Manchester. The latter coincidentally linked up geographically with East Midland's Frontrunner North West operations and thus placed the Scottish group in an enviable position.

Ribble's Manchester minibus subsidiary Bee Line had, a few days before passing to Stagecoach, signed an exclusive advertising deal with Imperial Tobacco under which cigarette advertising posters were applied to both sides of every vehicle in its 160-strong fleet. This was ironic in view of the total ban on smoking imposed by Hampshire Bus earlier in the year !

Having taken over the former United Transport Buses 'Zippy' operations in Preston and at a later date, UTB's Bee Line Buzz subsidiary in the Manchester area, Ribble had become Britain's largest minibus operator with a fleet of over 350 of these small vehicles. Their conventional fleet comprised mainly Leyland National single deckers, Leyland Leopard dual purpose vehicles and Bristol VRT, Leyland Atlantean and Olympian double deckers, a number of which had been purchased secondhand immediately following deregulation. Although the standard 'big bus' livery was red, grey and white, the minibus fleet in addition to using these colours also sported a yellow and red colour scheme, as did the vehicles from the two UTB fleets. The latter retained their Zippy and Bee Line Buzz fleet names whilst Ribble's own minibuses were operated under the Minilink banner, and the company's dual purpose vehicles, in white, red & grey used the Timesaver or Kingfisher fleet names. The company's fifteen depots were spread throughout Lancashire and south Cumbria whilst the head office and main repair works were centrally located at Preston.

Still seeking further consolidation, Stagecoach, through their Cumberland Motor Services subsidiary, acquired the cream & crimson-liveried 10-coach business of Cumbria independent operator Stephensons of Maryport on 2 May, immediately placing this under the control of its Kirkpatricks division. Stephenson's taxi and limousine hire business was however not included in the deal and remained with its original owner who also retained their existing premises in Maryport. Not all the inherited vehicles were used by their new owner and several coaches were immediately placed in

Still wearing the yellow, red & black livery and 'Zippy' fleet names of its former owner, United Transport Buses, Ribble 030 (D819PUK), a Carlyle-bodied Freight Rover Sherpa rests at Preston bus station and amusingly shows 'I'm zipping back to depot' on its destination blind. (J.Whitmore)

Ribble 900, seen here on Blackpool promenade still wearing NBC-style poppy red & white livery was the only Duple Dominant bus-bodied Leyland Tiger in the company's fleet. New in 1984, it had originally been acquired for evaluation purposes. (K.A.Jenkinson)

Stephenson's of Maryport OFR929T, a Duple-bodied Volvo B58-61 seen here at Morecambe in 1988 was acquired by Cumberland along with its owner's business in 1989 and was given fleet number 580. (T.W.W.Knowles)

Opposite page :
Left column, top to bottom :

East Midland Bristol VRT 186 in pre-Stagecoach group livery and wearing Mansfield & District fleet names arrives at Clipstone on crew-operated route 16 from Mansfield on 25 October 1990. The 16 service is more usually maintained by East Midland Routemasters. (K.A.Jenkinson)

Looking immaculate in its deep red & sandstone Carlislebus livery is Cumberland Routemaster 905 (WLT706), previously operated north of the border by Kelvin Scottish. Seen in Carlisle in January 1988, it is enroute to Morton Park on service 61. (K.A.Jenkinson)

Pictured in Blantyre soon after its entry into service and sporting UTM fleet names, former Kowloon Metsec-bodied Daimler CVG6 1002 passes UTM Leyland Victory Mk.2 369 in two-tone blue Cityline livery. (R.Bailey)

Typifying the double deck fleet of Fife Scottish is 829, an Alexander-bodied Ailsa Volvo seen here in Glenrothes bus station in April 1991. (K.A.Jenkinson)

Right column, top to bottom)

Passing Morecambe's Promenade Railway Station on 29 June 1988 is Ribble 617, a Robin Hood-bodied Iveco 49.10 sporting its owner's earlier style of Minilink fleet name. (K.A.Jenkinson)

Caught by the camera at Lightwater Valley Leisure Park, North Yorkshire on 10 June 1989, a few weeks after being acquired by Cumberland, Plaxton-bodied Leopard 561, still wearing the livery of its previous owner, Stephensons of Maryport, stands alongside Cumberland 105, a Duple Laser-bodied Leyland Tiger in National Holidays livery. (K.A.Jenkinson)

Passing through Stockport on its way to Hazel Grove in June 1989 is Bee Line Buzz Co. NCME-bodied Dodge S56 D417NNA. Adorned with an Embassy advert, it wears the silver & blue City Sprint livery in which it was delivered new. (K.A.Jenkinson)

Originally owned by Stagecoach, Plaxton-bodied Volvo LUA250V passed to Highwayman upon the formation of that company, later returning to the Stagecoach fold with the Errol-based business in February 1989. (K.A.Jenkinson)

After giving almost three years service to Magicbus in Glasgow, XSL596A (formerly 289CLT) was one of five Routemasters transferred to Stagecoach in September 1990 for operation in Perth. Resting between duties at Perth depot in April 1991, it carries a Perth Panther logo in the intermadiate apperture of its front destination screen. (K.A.Jenkinson)

17

store pending a decision on their future.

After several months of speculation as to its future following an approach in September 1988 by Ribble to purchase the ailing Barrow Borough Transport, the local authority-owned company was placed under administrative receivership on 21 December of that year. Seeing the position in which BBT now found itself led Ribble to increase its competition in the town in the hope that it might eventually succeed in its attempt to gain control of its rival, and as a result of renewed talks following the collapse of negotiations between Barrow and Holt Drive Hire of Bolton, this goal was achieved on 26 May. The £1.2million deal included Barrow Borough Transport's premises and all its 'owned' vehicles, but excluded BBT's van hire fleet or the right to trade as successors to Barrow Borough Transport. BBT's twelve leased Peugeot Talbot Pullman minibuses - which were also excluded from the deal - were returned to their rightful owner.

Following the takeover, immediate changes were made to Ribble's services to make up for BBT's disappearance but no additional routes were introduced and no extra vehicles were drafted in. Barrow's 24 buses - 11 Leyland Nationals, 6 Dodge S56 minibuses and 7 Leyland Atlanteans were temporarily removed from service although within days a couple of the Leyland Nationals were despatched to Preston where they were put to use by Ribble still wearing their former owner's cream & blue livery with the addition of Ribble fleet name vinyls. Ribble took two weeks to decide their new depot policy in Barrow and on 11 June moved their fleet from their Emlyn Street base to the premises acquired with the Barrow business at Hindpool Road. A week earlier, on 4 June, Ribble had vacated the premises of T.Brady in Ironworks Road, Barrow which they had used for the parking of vehicles.

Following an announcement by Ribble that they were to close their engineering works at Preston and undertake all maintenance at their major depots, they transferred all their Lakeland and South Cumbria operations to Cumberland Motor Services on 18 June. This included their depots at Barrow, Ulverston and Kendal and outstations at Grange over Sands and Sedbergh together with 114 vehicles, a number of which had been reshuffled immediately prior to their transfer taking place. To the casual onlooker, little had changed however and the vast majority of the ex.Ribble vehicles continued to sport their former owner's fleet names despite their change of ownership. Cumberland also took into stock an Alexander-bodied 27-seat Ford AO609 minibus from Smith of Dearham, Maryport following his withdrawal from stage carriage operation.

Throughout May and June, the now customary transfer of vehicles between Stagecoach's various subsidiaries had

Barrow Borough Transport's newest double decker was NCME-bodied Leyland Atlantean A266PEO which entered service in April 1984. Seen here at Barrow's Civic Centre in its original livery, this bus passed to Ribble with Barrow's operations etc. in 1989 and was given fleet number 1452 by its new owner. (D.J.Smithies)

Reeve Burgess-bodied Renault S56 coach-seated mini E779DEO of Barrow Borough Transport (with Barrovian Travel fleet names) prepares to leave the town centre on a stage carriage duty to Newbarns a few days before its municipal owners sank into financial difficulties. (T.W.W.Knowles)

continued unabated with Cumberland, in addition to gaining the vehicles mentioned above from Ribble, receiving back on 4 May the Ford Transit it had loaned to United Counties in December 1988. On the debit side, Cumberland loaned five of its Leyland Nationals to Ribble on 14 June and two Dodge S56 minibuses to Hampshire Bus from 24 June. The United Counties Routemaster (WLT980) which had been on loan to East Midland since April was permanently transferred to that company in May whilst more surprisingly, United Counties on 22 May despatched one of its Plaxton paramount 3500-bodied Leyland Tiger coaches - no.83 - to the recently-acquired United Transport Malawi.

Also purchased by Stagecoach Malawi from the Group's Hong Kong associate, Speedybus, were 12 Metsec-bodied Daimler CVG6s formerly operated by Kowloon Motor Bus Co. These were the first double deckers to be operated in Malawi and were shipped from Hong Kong to Durban snd then driven overland through Zimbabwe and Mozambique to Blantyre, a long and arduous journey.

Despite retaining its Ribble red & grey livery and fleet names, Leyland National 863 was owned by Cumberland when this photograph was taken in Duke Street, Barrow in Furness in October 1990 following the transfer of Ribble's south Lakeland operations to Cumberland Motor Services. (D.J.Smithies)

Back at home, Ribble loaned one of its Freight Rover Sherpa minibuses to local Blackburn inderpendent J.Haydock from 4 to 12 June and three former Barrow Dodge S56s to East Midland for two months while Hampshire Bus loaned one of its Dennis Javelin buses to Tillingbourne of Cranleigh from 27 June to 6 July. Prior to this date, another of Hampshire Bus's Javelins - 802 - was severely damaged in an accident on 2 June and had to be returned to Duple for rebuilding. A trio of East Midland Leyland Nationals moved south to join Hampshire Bus who scrapped one of its two Leyland-DAB bendi-buses during this same month.

North of the border, Stagecoach were preparing - amidst great secrecy - for an attack on Strathtay Scottish who were at that time in line to be the first Scottish Bus Group company to be offered for sale in the SBG privatisation and began to amass a quantity of Leyland Nationals which were transferred from Hampshire Bus (8) and United Counties (1) in May and Cumberland (5) and East Midland (5) in June. Also received, albeit on loan, from Hampshire Bus was a Bristol FLF6G Lodekka which had been converted for driver training purposes and wore an all-yellow livery, this being in preparation for training the large number of extra drivers that would be needed for the assault on Strathtay. Taken out of service during May and June were a trio of Alexander-bodied Leyland Leopards, one of which was immediately sold to an operator in Coatbridge while the other two were placed in store to await a decision on their future. The Routemaster fleet was further reduced when five examples left the 'graveyards' at Carlisle and Spittalfield. Three of these were dispersed for scrap whilst the other two - including the low bridge victim - were sold to a preservationist for spares.

In Glasgow, Magicbus introduced changes to its service 19 to Easterhouse on Tuesday 30 May, with the evening service after 7.00pm operating on a 20-minute frequency. More importantly however, all the evening journeys were from that date to be one person operated with the result that the Routemasters which normally maintained the 19 had to be replaced after the early evening peak each day. To enable the introduction of one person operation, a further four ex.Devon General Bristol VRTs were acquired and allocated to Glasgow depot and as well as being used in the evenings, these buses were also often to be seen, crew operated, on the Easterhouse route at other times of the day.

Having chosen Hampshire Bus to evaluate the Group's new Dennis Javelin buses, it came as no surprise when Cumberland was selected as recipients of some Leyland Lynx single deckers in view of the company's close proximity to Leyland's factory at Workington. The first to arrive was a Leyland demonstrator which arrived in June, a few days before the company's three new Lynx's were delivered. The latter were however not placed in service until the following month when they took up their duties at Barrow in Furness where they were used to convert a former minibus route to conventional bus operation. Cumberland also borrowed an Optare Delta demonstrator from its manufacturer, using this in service from 14 June to 5 July.

Following the temporary loss of Dennis Javelin 802 following its involvement in an accident, Hampshire Bus Leyland National 747 sustained severe damage in an accident at Longwood Cross Roads on 23 June while operating a duty on the 93 service and as a result was withdrawn for cannibalisation. As a temporary replacement,

Resting in the sunshine at Magicbus's Warroch Street depot, Glasgow on 21 August 1989 are former Devon general Bristol VRTs 109, 105 & 103 (FDV840/16/0V). Despite having been in service for some weeks, none have yet received Magicbus destination blinds or fleet names. (S.A.Jenkinson)

One of a large number of Alexander-bodied Leyland Leopards acquired from Kelvin Scottish in 1987, all-white liveried XGM460L in Buchanan bus station, Glasgow on 27 March 1989 was working Magicbus's service 19 to Easterhouse as indicated by its windscreen labels. After its withdrawal from service it spent several months in use as a uniform store at Stagecoach's Inveralmond depot, Perth before eventually being sold for scrap. (Murdoch Currie)

Below : 252, one of Cumberland's Leyland Lynx buses stands at the Ormsgill terminus of Barrow local service 2 to West Shore, Walney Island in 1990, clearly showing its coloured destination blind. (D.J.Smithies)

a Duple bus-bodied Dennis Javelin demonstrator was borrowed from Yeates (dealers), Loughborough on 27 June and this remained with Hampshire Bus until 6 July. The company also acquired a Robin Hood-bodied Iveco 49.10 minibus from United Counties whilst a pair of Leyland Leopard coaches were transferred from East Midland to their subsidiary, Rainworth Travel in June.

As a result of the inability of Scottish Bus Group subsidiary Central Scottish to operate their services due to continued strike action by their employees, Magicbus introduced a new service, numbered 53, from Buchanan bus station in Glasgow to Birkenshaw and Larkhall a few days before the Central strike ended on 27 May. The temporary operations on the 53 ended when Central's buses again took to the roads, but having found this service to be reasonably lucrative, Magicbus registered it for regular operation to commence on 3 July. Meanwhile, on 1 May, Stagecoach had revamped their services from Edinburgh and Glasgow to Aberdeen and had added a 'Breakfast Express' journey from Aberdeen to Glasgow each morning and a 'Supper Express' journey in the return direction each evening. On these, which operated seven days a week, a full range of hot meals were available onboard ranging from 85p for a burger to £1.70 for a full 'airline' breakfast and the normal fare of £6.50 single was applied. At this same time, all the Anglo-Scottish journeys were upgraded to 'Super Service' and in conjunction with a service provided by ABC Travel supported by Buckinghamshire County Council, a free connecting service was provided from junction 14 on the M1 motorway to Milton Keynes. As a result of its ever increasing popularity, Magicbus's nightly Londonlink service was also expanded by the introduction of a daytime operation.

Still carrying its cartoon character 'The Tourist' - a remnant of the Torbay Free Bus operation - on its front panel despite having gained Stagecoach-style livery, Hampshire Bus Leyland National 747 prepares to leave Winchester depot to take up its duties in August 1988.   (Ian Buck)

In southern England, Hampshire Bus participated in the 'Sunday Rider' scheme introduced by Hampshire County Council in which a county-wide ticket provided travel throughout the county on the buses of fifteen operators and three ferry services. A family ticket was available at a cost of £5.50 (2 adults and 2 children) or an adult ticket could be purchased for £2.75 or child/OAP for £2. Launched on 21 May, the 'Sunday Rider' scheme continued until 3 September and was to prove extremely popular, attracting numerous additional passengers to the previously under-used Sunday bus services.

Returning to Scotland, Magicbus's recently-acquired ex.Devon General Bristol VRTs began to oust Routemasters from some of their usual Glasgow haunts, and became an increasingly familiar sight particularly on the 20 service to Castlemilk where they were crew operated. More surprising however was the announcement by Stagecoach of a number of new stage carriage services in the Perth area where Scottish Bus Group subsidiary Strathtay Scottish reigned supreme. In many circles, it had been thought that an attack on Strathtay would have been launched in 1986 at the time of deregulation and thus, when news broke of Stagecoach's impending assault, it came as a complete surprise to all except a very few who had been privy to the secret plans for the new services in Tayside.

Meanwhile, Stagecoach in June began a programme of full-day tours from various points in Tayside to a number of areas of scenic beauty, running these through the summer season until mid-September. On Mondays the tour travelled through Braemar where a stop was made at a famous knitwear factory, Cairnwell Summit, Glenshee and Ballater while on Tuesday it crossed Scotland via the Tay Bridge, Kincardine Bridge and Helensburgh to Luss and Balloch and included a cruise on Loch Lomond. Wednesday'sTour travelled northwards to Killiecrankie, Drumochter, Inverness, Fort Augustus and Dalwhinnie with visits to Culloden Battlefield, Cawdor Castle and the Loch Ness Visitors Centre while on Thursday the itinerary included Lochearnhead, Crianlarich, Tyndrum and Oban, a three hour stay being scheduled in the latter town. Leaving the various Tayside picking up points at 8.30 - 9.30am, these tours arrived home before 8.00pm and cost between £8.80 and £11.90. with reductions for OAPs and children. A novel feature of these days out was that the price charged included admission charges (where applicable) to the places visited and in addition, lunch and afternoon tea which was served on the coach. Although occasionally single deck coaches were used, more often it was the company's luxurious Neoplan Skyliners which undertook these tours, thus affording passengers superb views of the countryside through which they passed.

Opposite page :
Left column, top to bottom :

Seen in Preston bus station a few days before Ribble's acquisition of Mercers of Grimsargh's operations is NKU563R, an ex.South Yorkshire PTE East Lancs-bodied Daimler Fleetline. (Travelscene)

Acquired by Stagecoach from Inverness Traction along with that company's operations was Alexander-bodied Leopard L14 (HSC802N) pictured here at its home depot in November 1989.

Southdown Leyland National 43 (RUF43R) in its owner's traditional apple green & cream livery was actually operating for Top Line when photographed in March 1990. As can be seen, yellow Top Line names had been added on its front panel and in the nearside windscreen.   (Ian Buck)

Cumberland 103, a Duple-bodied Leyland Tiger sports its owner's yellow & tan Coachline livery as it stands at Barrow depot on 7 March 1991 after working an Asda shoppers contract. (B.K.Pritchard)

Right column, top to bottom :

Still sporting Ribble's Kingfisher livery, former National Travel West Plaxton-bodied Leopard 76 (MRJ276W) basks in the sunshine in Blackpool whilst on a private hire duty.   (K.A.Jenkinson)

Painted in the old Hampshire Mini Bus livery of silver, red & blue, Robin Hood-bodied Iveco 49.10 39 awaits its passengers in Andover bus station. (Ian Buck)

Although still wearing Top Line's yellow & black livery, former Eastbourne Buses East Lancs-bodied Atlantean RHC727S had, by March 1990, received Hastings fleet names after joining Stagecoach-owned Hastings & District.   (Ian Buck)

United Counties operated Routemasters in Bedford and Corby. WLT 980 seen here in the latter town was later loaned to East Midland who after a short while permanently added it to their fleet.

PERTH PANTHER ON THE ATTACK

The build up by Stagecoach of a large fleet of Leyland Nationals drawn from their subsidiary fleets south of the border signified that a major battle was being planned and this proved to be true when the first wave entered service on 19 June. Operating two services across Perth from North Muirton to Letham on a 7/8 minute frequency, these, lettered 'A' and 'B', shadowed Strathtay's most lucrative routes and offered cheaper fares. The buses used were given 'Perth Panther' fleet names and logos, had a stylised route diagram painted on their roof edges and destination details painted onto the glass of their front destination box. The introduction of these new predatory services not surprisingly brought an immediate response from Strathtay Scottish who, on 3 July, introduced a new service - numbered 4 - between Perth city centre and Letham which matched the frequency of the Stagecoach 'Panther' route. In addition, Strathtay repainted six of its ex. London Routemasters into the old Perth City Transport livery of red

Before any further moves were made north of the border, East Midland, who were finding it increasingly difficult to maintain their southern base due to it being some 150 or so miles away from its main area of operation, sold Frontrunner South East to Ensign Bus of Purfleet on 30 June. Although Frontrunner's seven services and depots at Wyatts Green; Debden; Rainham and Roneo Corner, Romford all passed to Ensign Bus, the Wyatts Green and Debden bases along with the four rural Essex County Council services were immediately 'sold on' to County Coach & Bus of Harlow, a company derived from the old London Country North East concern. In reality, despite not officially taking over until 30 June, Ensign had helped to operate services 248 and 252 and schools service 550 during the week prior to the official takeover date due to the unavailability of crews and servicable vehicles by Frontrunner, although for the final day of operations, East Midland sent its Routemaster WLT980 - which had by now gained its new owner's two-tone green &

Former Cumberland Leyland National MAO369P was transferred to Stagecoach for use on the new Perth Panther services. Seen here at Walnut Grove depot, Perth on 8 July 1989, it had its route details painted onto its front destination glass and also carried a stylised route map painted onto its cove panels. (Murdoch Currie)

& cream and added to these the 'Perth City Transport' fleetname, giving the impression to passengers that two new bus operators had appeared on the streets of Perth whereas in reality, only one was new !

Meanwhile, Neil Renilson, Strathtay's managing director resigned his position to enable him to take up a senior executive position with Stagecoach in September 1989. His knowledge of Strathtay's operations and policies obviously proved invaluable to his new masters and greatly assisted them in their future plans towards expansion on Tayside.

cream livery - to Essex to work the 248 route. At the time of its sale to Ensign Bus, Frontrunner South East's fleet comprised 30 former Greater Manchester Atlanteans and although all of these were loaned to Ensign Bus from 30 June, it was agreed that they would not be retained long term and would be exchanged for a similar number of dual-door double deckers from within the Stagecoach Group as soon as was possible. This exchange was undertaken over a period of time in July and August when a total of 23 Leyland Atlanteans and 8 Bristol VRTs were acquired by Ensign from Ribble together with 4 Bristol REs from East Midland. In

Typifying the 'bus war' in Perth in its early stages, Stagecoach's Perth Panther Leyland National 214 (GTL352N) operating route B to Letham passes a Strathtay Scottish Perth City Transport-liveried Routemaster (SR3 - WTS329A) in Kinnoull Street, Perth on 21 August 1989. (K.A.Jenkinson)

Above : One of four ECW-bodied coach-seated Bristol RELH6Ls operated by East Midland at the time of its acquisition by tStagecoach, 5 (NNN5M) of 1974 vintage looks immaculate in its two-tone green & cream livery. (East Midland)

Both sporting Perth Panther fleet names in Kinnoull Street, Perth on 21 August 1989, Leyland National 211 (GFX975N) on town service D to Moncreiffe passes Plaxton-bodied Volvo 401 (LUB508P) which has just arrived from Comrie on the 15 service. (S.A.Jenkinson)

growing share of the market in Perth, Stagecoach - again under their Perth Panther banner - began a new hourly service from the city centre to Pitcairngreen in direct competition to Strathtay, and on this employed Leyland Leopard and Volvo coaches from the Stagecoach fleet which were suitably adorned with Perth Panther lettering and logos. All the new services ran on a Monday to Saturday basis, leaving Strathtay to retain their supremacy only on Sundays. Determined to fight back, Strathtay repainted a couple of its Leyland Leopards into a new livery upon which the legend 'This is the *Pitcairn* GREEN BUS' was added to each side ! At this same time, Stagecoach were registering a new Tayside area bus service each week, a practice which continued for some two months. The effect on morale at Strathtay Scottish at the weekly announcement of what route Stagecoach had registered that week was dramatic !

return, Ribble received the 30 Frontrunner ex. Greater Manchester Atlanteans, most of which visited East Midland's workshops on their journey north.

Returning to Scotland, Stagecoach had allocated fleet numbers to all their buses and coaches and these began to appear on the vehicles concerned towards the end of June. Surprisingly, the new numbering scheme even included a number of vehicles which, being heavily cannibalised, seemed unlikely to ever be used in service.

Having now firmly established their first two 'Perth Panther' services, Stagecoach launched a further attack on Strathtay Scottish by introducing another competitive route on 17 July. Operating on a figure 9 basis from William Lows Superstore via Tulloch, Perth city centre and Moncrieffe, clockwise journeys were lettered 'C' whilst those operating anti-clockwise were lettered 'D'. Both ran every fifteen minutes giving a combined 7½ minute frequency between the city centre and Tulloch. Again using Leyland Nationals, some of which had a stylised route diagram painted on their roof edges, these like services 'A' and 'B' operated on a flat fare basis with a charge of 30p (15p for children and 10p for Tayside pass-holders) and also accepted the Panther Pass, a £3.25 weekly ticket which permitted unlimited travel and could be purchased on the bus. Not content with their

To challenge Perth Panther on the service to Pitcairngreen, Strathtay Scottish painted some of its Duple-bodied Leopard coaches into a special livery to which the legend 'This is the Pitcairn *Green Bus' was added. Demonstrating this is SL28 (YJU694), arriving at Kinnoull Street Perth on the competing service on 21 August 1989.   (K.A.Jenkinson)*

As yet still to receive its fleet number 412 but sporting Perth Panther fleet names, Volvo B58-61 JSR42X which was fitted with a new Duple body in December 1987 is seen in Kinnoull Street, Perth on 21 August 1989 having just arrived on the 15 service from Comrie.   (S.K.Jenkinson)

Cumberland's ECW-bodied Leyland Atlantean 1425, still in Ribble's red & grey livery albeit with its new owner's fleet names, prepares to leave Duke Street, Barrow in Furness in October 1990 on a peak-hour journey to North Scale on Walney Island, a route normally maintained by minibuses. (D.J.Smithies)

Wearing Cumberland's immediate pre-Stagecoach livery of dark red with a sandstone roof upon which the title 'CMS Cumberland' was carried, Leyland National 2 394 rests near Kirkpatrick's depot at Brigham in August 1988. (K.A.Jenkinson)

Freshly repainted into Stagecoach-style corporate livery, Cumberland Leyland National 369 stands outside Workington depot on 11 April 1989 with an NFS (not for service) label affixed to its windscreen. (A.Gilmour)

Amongst Stagecoach's English subsidiaries, Cumberland during July converted more of their Barrow town services from minibus to conventional bus operation while East Midland undertook a major revision of their services to eliminate competition between their own company and its subsidiary, Rainworth Travel. As a result, Rainworth's services 22, 82, 87 and 88 which had been operated under tender from Nottinghamshire County Council were, upon their expiry in July, replaced by new commercial services and a new Rainworth route (75) was started from Worksop to Mansfield via Whitwell, Creswell, Langwith and Warsop as a replacement for their service 77 and the off-peak East Midland 76 route. Ribble finally closed its central repair works at Frenchwood Avenue, Preston in mid-July and after that time, all repair work was transferred to the company's main depots and to Cumberland's depots at Kendal and Barrow. The competition faced by Cumberland in Kendal was eliminated when Lancaster City Transport withdrew its town services on 29 July, although the latter continued to operate its hourly service to Ambleside, thus retaining a presence in the area.

Overseas, a further 8 ex.Kowloon Moror Bus Daimler CVG6 double deckers had arrived in Malawi during June to bring the total of this type to 20, although it was not until 25 July that the first two made their debut in service. These were put to use on the busy Blantyre - Limbe - Kamuzu Highway corridor and at first were viewed with some trepidation by passengers who appeared extremely reluctant to travel on the upper deck. It seemed that their fright was caused by the fact that they did not know to where the stairs led, and, after reaching the upper deck this phobia was heightened by them ' not being able to see the driver'.

Happily, such fears appear to have been short lived, and within a few weeks, the upper deck proved as popular amongst passengers as was the lower saloon. As was to be expected, a repainting programme was quickly put in hand to transform the UTM fleet into Stagecoach corporate livery, although the local and regional identity fleet names such as Cityline, Coachline, Expressline and Southern etc. were retained. Additionally, vehicles of the various divisions were given different coloured front roof domes in order to maintain ease of identification to would-be passengers.

One of a number of tri-axle Talbot Pullman minibuses acquired by Ribble from United Transport's 'Zippy' fleet, yellow & red liveried 078 (E737UNA) is seen here after receiving standard Ribble Minilink fleet names. (T.W.W.Knowles)

July proved to be a most eventful month as far as Stagecoach's combined fleet was concerned and in addition to witnessing the arrival of a number of new buses and coaches, several were moved round amongst the various subsidiaries to cater for their differing needs. In Scotland, six new Robin Hood-bodied Iveco 49.10 minibuses were received on the 15th of the month and were immediately allocated to Perth Panther duties which they shared with the Leyland Nationals. Two of the new Ivecos however, quickly departed to United Counties to whom they were temporarily loaned, returning to Perth the following month. Meanwhile four new Plaxton Paramount-bodied Volvo B10M-20 48-seat coaches with onboard toilets were added to the Stagecoach fleet for use on the company's long distance services. A further Leyland National was received from East Midland to supplement the Panther fleet, this bearing the signwritten legend 'Best Wishes to Perth Panther from East Midland' on its rear roof dome, whilst leaving Perth was the ex.Highwayman Whittaker-bodied Mercedes L608D minicoach which was sent on loan to Hampshire Bus. Another of the ex.Kelvin Leopards was withdrawn from service and placed in reserve while five Leopards - including one which had never been used by Stagecoach - were sold to SBG Engineering or Dunsmore (breaker), Larkhall. Three former London Routemasters also left the reserve fleet at Spittalfield when two departed to a South Yorkshire breaker and the other was sold to a byuer in Norway.

South of the border, Cumberland despatched a pair of its Dodge S56 minibuses and a Mercedes L709D on loan to Hampshire Bus who also gained a 29-seat Dormobile-bodied Mercedes 709D from its bodybuilder for three weeks evaluation from 26 July to 19 August. Hampshire Bus took its remaining Leyland-DAB bendi-bus out of service and placed it in store until a decision was made as to its future while

United Counties received four new 85-seat Alexander-bodied Leyland Olympians - painted in the Group's corporate livery -, these being joined by a further six at the start of the following month.

Responding to an appeal made on BBC television's 'Challenge Anneka' programme, East Midland generously donated one of their older Bristol VRTs to the National Playbus Association and together with nine double deckers from other operators, this was quickly transformed into its new role in full view of the television cameras with the help of some of East Midland's employees.

As has been mentioned earlier, the 30 former Frontrunner South East Atlanteans were gradually returned to Ribble from Ensign Bus during July and August in exchange for a number of Atlanteans and Bristol VRTs from the Ribble fleet and upon their arrival back in Lancashire, most were

One of two Leyland-DAB bendi-buses operated by Hampshire Bus, 291 returns to Winchester from Southampton on 23 July 1988. (Ian Buck)

Pressed into service by Ribble still wearing its Frontrunner South East two-tone green & cream livery, former Greater Manchester NCME-bodied Leyland Atlantean 1663 (JND984N), which has gained red 'Ribble' fleet names, almost hides a red & grey-liveried Leyland National outside Blackburn depot on 25 October 1989.
(K.A.Jenkinson)

immediately placed in service at Bolton and Blackburn garages still wearing their former owner's two-tone green & cream livery. Indeed, some still sported London Bus roundels following their use on LRT contracted services in Essex, although these were removed after a few days and gradually each bus was given Ribble fleet names in place of those carried upon their arrival in their 'new' home.

Three new Alexander-bodied Leyland Olympians of United Counties pose for the camera in Bedford bus station. On the left, coach-seated 648 & 649 carry Coachlinks fleet names whilst on the right is a standard bus-seated example. (G.T.W.Carter)

SCOTLAND-LONDON LONDON-SCOTLAND WITH SUPER STAGECOACH

NEW FOR SUMMER 1989
PIPING HOT MEALS
50p Voucher enclosed

★ SUPER DAY & NIGHT SERVICES — NOW FULLY UPGRADED TO SUPER SERVICE FOR LESS THAN OUR OLD SUPER SERVICE FARE
★ FREE CONNECTING BUS LINK TO CENTRAL MILTON KEYNES

FROM EXPRESS TO STAGE CARRIAGE

August had barely begun when it was surprisingly and unexpectedly announced that Stagecoach had sold its entire express coach operation, its headquarters at Walnut Grove, Perth and a number of vehicles to National Express to enable total concentration to be given to its stage carriage interests throughout Britain and overseas. The deal, signed on 4 August, allowed National Express to use the Stagecoach name for a period of two years in order to assist it in establishing itself in Scotland, although a subsidiary company was set up under the title of Caledonian Express to take over the Stagecoach operations. Also in the deal was a clause which allowed Stagecoach Holdings the continued use of their Walnut Grove offices and depot until alternative accommodation could be found. A total of 31 coaches comprising 15 Volvos, 9 Neoplan Skyliners, 3 Neoplan Jetliners and the 4 Magicbus DAFs were sold to Caledonian Express together with the burnt-out ex.Amberline Neoplan which had been used for spares and an ex.Hampshire Bus Leyland recovery wagon, Stagecoach's two remaining Neoplan Skyliners having been sold to tours operator Yau Fung in Hong Kong a few days earlier.

Despite wearing full Stagecoach livery and fleet names, Plaxton Paramount-bodied Volvo B10M-61 5142SC (originally A799TGG and later A613TCR) was operating for Hampshire Bus when caught by the camera in August 1988 on tour in Whitby. (K.A.Jenkinson)

Standing at Walnut Grove depot, Perth on 21 August 1989, Neoplan Skyliner A394XGG awaits despatch to its new owner in Hong Kong while former Hampshire Bus Leyland recovery wagon FRN805W and Plaxton-bodied Volvo D442CNR, despite their fleet names, had become the property of Tayside Travel Services (Caledonian Express). (S.K.Jenkinson)

Seen at Walnut Grove depot, Perth on 27 October 1989 in the livery of its new owner, Tayside Travel Services (Caledonian Express) and complete with Stagecoach fleet names, is Neoplan Jetliner 4585SC which began life as A216LWD and was later re-registered A544XGG. (K.A.Jenkinson)

As a result of the sale of their express coaching interests, Stagecoach Holdings made arrangements to place all their Scottish stage carriage operations under their Magic Bus (Scotland) Ltd. banner and following the transfer of all their service licences to the latter-named company, a start was made in applying Magicbus legal lettering to all the company's Perth-based vehicles. The Magicbus fleet name however, was not to be carried other than by the Glasgow fleet, and on Tayside the Stagecoach name was to remain unaltered for the ex.McLennan services while Perth Panther was used for the new competitive services against Strathtay.

Stagecoach's unrelenting battle with Strathtay escalated on 7 August when a new Monday to Saturday service, numbered 15, was started from Perth to Crieff and Comrie. With a journey time of 57 minutes, this hourly service was operated mainly by Leyland Leopard or Volvo coaches, most of which by now carried Perth Panther fleet names. A week later, on 12 August, two more services were introduced in Perth, these operating on a circular basis between Scone and Burghmuir and passing through the city centre. Lettered E and F, and each running every 20 minutes to provide a combined 10-minute headway, these routes - which once

Left : One of Stagecoach's first minibuses, Perth Panther-liveried Robin Hood-bodied Iveco 022 (F22PSL) leaves Kinnoull Street, Perth on its way to Hillend on service E on 21 August 1989. In February 1990, this bus, along with a number of its sisters was transferred to Southdown in whose fleet it was numbered 924 before moving on to join Hampshire Bus in January 1991.   (K.A.Jenkinson)

Below : The Perth Panther Cub fleet name as fitted to the Robin Hood-bodied Iveco 49.10 minibuses. (S.K.Jenkinson)

Left : Strathtay Scottish introduced a number of Dormobile-bodied Renault S56 minibuses to Perth in 1989 in order to compete with Perth Panther's incursion into the city. Operating under Strathtay's 'City Nipper' banner, SS15 is seen here in its red, ivory & black livery.   (K.A.Jenkinson)

again competed with Strathtay Scottish - were operated by Robin Hood-bodied Iveco 49.10 minibuses carrying 'Perth Panther Cub' fleet names. Hail and Ride facilities were applicable on Oakbank Road and Muircroft Drive, Burghmuir and to publicise these new routes, all passengers were carried free of charge on the first two days of operation and adverts which proclaimed 'At Last ! A decent bus service for Scone and Burghmuir' were placed in the local newspapers. Determined not to lose the 'war', Strathtay replaced a number of its Perth-based conventional buses with new 25-seat Dormobile-bodied Renault S56s painted in an updated version of the crimson & cream Perth City Transport livery, placing these in service under the 'City Nipper' title.

During this period of attrition on Tayside, Stagecoach further strengthened its position on the south coast of England when, on 16 August, it purchased Southdown Motor Services from under the nose of Alan Stephenson's AJS Holdings who had been attempting to add this important

operator to its portfolio for several weeks. The acquisition of Southdown, whose western boundary butted up to Hampshire Bus added not only a further 250 or so vehicles to the Group's combined fleet, but also gave them a wide area of operation which stretched from Hasings to beyond Southampton. Included in the deal was Southdown's subsidiary, Sharpton, which owned all the company's depots, offices and bus stations, and Southdown's 51% share in Hastings Top Line Buses Ltd., a company formed in 1987 by Southdown and Eastbourne Buses. Within days of gaining control of Southdown, Stagecoach Holdings - as could have been expected - acquired Eastbourne's 49% stake in Top Line, thus gaining total control of that company. Rather than merge Top Line into the Southdown company as one would have imagined, it was instead retained as a separate operation but was placed under their control for administrative purposes.

In Lancashire, Ribble began a programme of

Still sporting Southdown's pre-Stagecoach apple green & cream livery and carrying advertising posters on its side and front is Leyland National 113, seen here in the late summer of 1990. (J.A.Godwin)

Above : Painted in Southdown's traditional apple green & cream livery, Bristol VRT 687 passes Hilsea depot a few months before Stagecoach gained control of the company.   (B.Newsome)

Above right : Passing along Hastings sea front on 6 March 1990 on its way to Harrow Lane is Leyland National MOD822P which sports the original style Top Line yellow livery with black window frames and skirt.   (Ian Buck)

Right : Illustrating Top Line's later livery which omitted the black skirt and had its fleet name repositioned on the cove panels, 22 (BCD822L) also carries a tiny green Southdown sticker above its front fleet name. It is seen here at Hastings on 6 March 1990 enroute to Tesco's superstore at Hollington.   (Ian Buck)

Right : Collecting its passengers in Lancaster bus station in yellow, red & black Minilink livery is Ribble 567, one of a pair of Carlyle-bodied 21-seat Freight Rover Sherpa minibuses purchased in 1989.   (T.W.W.Knowles)

Although the Tay Tiger fleet name was applied to Leyland National 209 (GFX973N), it never entered service in this form and after only a couple of days, its new identity was removed to leave only traces on its side panels of what had previously adorned them. (Campbell Morrison)

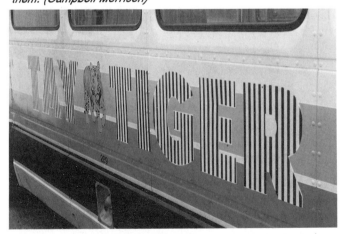

reorganisation in respect of its minibus routes in the Preston area where increasing competition was being experienced following the expansion by Preston Transport of their minibus fleet and the intrusion by the latter into areas previously regarded as Ribble strongholds. Several Ribble minibus routes, including some of the Zippy operations acquired from UTB, were deregistered, whilst others were closely monitored to assess their future viability.

Back in Scotland, the battle with Strathtay Scottish continued and on 21 August an attack was mounted on Dundee where Stagecoach inaugurated a new service from the city centre to Monifieth in direct competition to Strathtay's identical 75 service. Cheekily, Stagecoach numbered their new service 75, and operated this with Leyland Nationals. Although it was originally planned that this new service was to use the 'Tay Tigers' brand name, the vehicles employed at the last minute had their Tay Tigers fleet names removed and replaced with the Stagecoach name after Tayside Buses, the Dundee municipal operator, signed a sponsorship deal with the Tayside Tigers ice hockey team a couple of days before the new 75 service was due to commence. As stocks of Tay Tiger tickets had however already been printed, these were used, despite their reference to a fleet name which never appeared elsewhere. A week later, a second service was launched in Dundee, this being the 74 from the city centre to Carnoustie which shadowed the Strathtay route bearing the same number. Accommodation for Stagecoach's small Dundee-based fleet was provided by Greyhound Coaches at their East Dock Street premises, close to the Tayside Regional Transport depot, although this was purely for parking purposes and Stagecoach's vehicles continued to return to Spittalfield or Perth for maintenance. Meanwhile, in Glasgow, Magicbus had withdrawn their short-lived 53 service to Larkhall on 6 August after finding this not to be as profitable as had been originally anticipated.

A new addition to the Stagecoach family came into the world on 22 August when Brian Souter's wife, Betty gave birth to a daughter, Amy. This gave the company's chairman

Stagecoach's solitary B-series Leyland National, ex.Ribble TRN811V passes Seagate bus station, Dundee on 21 August 1989 whilst operating service 75 which shadowed Strathtay Scottish's route bearing that same number.
(K.A.Jenkinson)

Unique within Stagecoach's combined fleet is Yugoslavian-bodied Famos-Ensign Charisma coach G100JNV. Operated by United Counties and wearing National Express livery, it leaves Luton bus station in October 1989 on a National Express-contracted service 325 to Leeds & Bradford.   (T.G.Walker)

even greater pleasure than Stagecoach's previous year's trading results which showed a pre-tax profit of £3,458,000 on a turnover of £36,757,000 on the year to 30 April 1989. Also joining the ever expanding Stagecoach empire was a six-seater Cessna light aircraft, purchased for use mainly by the Group directors to enable them to more speedily visit their scattered outposts. Housed at Scone airfield near Perth, in true Stagecoach manner the plane was obtained in exchange for a batch of six buses !

On the vehicle front, August saw the arrival of nine more new Robin Hood-bodied Iveco minibuses for use by Stagecoach on its Perth Panther operations whilst Hampshire Bus received a trio of new Alexander-bodied, coach-seated Leyland Olympians. More unusual was the purchase for United Counties of a Famos S315.21 coach sold in the UK as the 'Ensign Charisma' and possibly obtained as part of the deal involving the disposal of the Frontrunner South East operations. The coach was used on National Express contracted services and was painted in that company's Rapide livery. Inter-fleet transfers found United Counties gaining two Cumberland minibuses - a Dodge S56 and a Mercedes L709D - from Hampshire Bus to whom they had been on loan and a trio of Hampshire Bus Freight Rover Sherpas while Cumberland loaned a pair of Mellor-bodied Ford Tranits to East Midland's subsidiary, Rainworth Travel. These were destined to be the only vehicles to carry full Stagecoach livery and Rainworth Travel fleet names. Stagecoach borrowed a Mercedes minibus from Cumberland from 13 August until 1 September for use at Perth and although this was intended only for use as a staff shuttle bus to ferry crews from the city centre to the depot at Walnut

Grove, it was used on several occasions on the city's Panther Cub services. More unusual was the hire by Cumberland of a MCW-bodied Leyland PD3A/1 driver trainer from Blackpool Transport for temporary use in this same role

One of only two vehicles to carry Rainworth Travel fleet names on Stagecoach corporate livery was former Cumberland Mellor-bodied Ford Transit D639VAO, seen here in the shadows of Shirebrook depot in October 1990.   (Travelscene)

Accident damaged Bristol Lodekka 082 (GDL771E) which had served Stagecoach from October 1984 until September 1989 is seen being dismantled at Spittalfield depot on 13 March 1990. (S.A.Jenkinson)

Having now had time to assess the position at Southdown, it was announced that the company's depots at Horsham and Haywards Heath which had been closed prior to the Stagecoach take-over were now regarded as being surplus to requirements and were to be sold at an early date while no decision was taken as to the future of the recently-closed depot at Hayling Island. Some weeks later, on 24 September, Top Line's Wayfarer ticket machines were all replaced by Almex 'A' machines provided by Southdown and on the following day, Southdown purchased the stage carriage operations and vehicles of Cedar Travel, Worthing. This provided Southdown with six additional services in Worthing and eight more minibuses - 5 MCW Metroriders and 3 Iveco Dailybuses - which were immediately moved to Southdown's depot in that town. It was intended that Cedar would be operated as a subsidiary division and that its white, orange & brown livery and fleet name would be retained. Cedar's coaching interests were not included in this deal however and remained with their original owner.

In the meantime, most of Top Line's Eastbourne Buses Atlantean double deckers had, on 24 September, been returned to their rightful owner and replaced by Leyland Nationals drawn from the Southdown fleet and only two Atlanteans now remained, these being required for use on heavily-loaded schools journeys. The new arrivals all retained their Southdown green & cream livery and fleet names and were not repainted into Top Line's yellow & black colours.

Continuing its vigourous activities towards rationalisation, Stagecoach sold its Ribble subsidiary, Bee Line Buzz, the majority of Ribble's operations in Manchester and its East Midland's subsidiary, Frontrunner North West to the Drawlane Group on 30 September. This included 186 minibuses and 44 conventional buses and coaches from Ribble and Bee Line, depots at Stockport, Tintwhistle and Manchester, and most of the services from these with the exception of a small handful which were transferred to Ribble at Bolton. Although not included in the deal, in the short term, Drawlane were to continue using Frontrunner's vehicles based at Tintwhistle until suitable replacements could be drafted in. As part of the agreement reached between Stagecoach and Drawlane in respect of this

from 11 August while Hampshire Bus inspected and road tested a DAF-Optare Delta at Winchester on 3 August although it was not used in service. Unfortunately, Hampshire Bus' Dennis Javelin 802, which had been returned to service on 26 July after undergoing accident repairs at Duple's Hendon premises, was involved in an accident at Romsey on 26 August which led to it having once again to be despatched to Duple for attention. Another collision victim was Stagecoach Bristol FLF6G Lodekka GDL771E which sustained severe frontal damage and as a result was withdrawn for cannibalisation. Two more of Stagecoach's rapidly diminishing fleet of Leyland Leopards were sold and one of the company's FS6G Lodekkas which, since its arrival from Hampshire Bus in March 1988 had remained out of use at Spittalfield, was sold to a driver training concern.

Eastbourne Buses East Lancs-bodied Leyland Atlantean 32 (YJK932V) was one of the first buses to be painted in the yellow & black Top Line livery in May 1988. Following Stagecoach's acquisition of Eastbourne's share of the Top Line operation, this bus was added to the Southdown fleet where it was numbered 356. (Eastbourne Buses)

Painted in Southdown's apple green & cream livery but carrying Top Line fleet names, Leyland National 26 (PCD126M) stands alongside yellow & black-liveried Top Line Leyland National MOD822P at the company's Hastings depot in November 1989. (Ian Buck)

transaction, Drawlane subsidiary, North Western, who had since June 1988 been competing with Ribble on a number of services in the Blackburn area, withdrew from the fray on 11 September and passed the services concerned to Ribble. Technically, Ribble loaned vehicles to North Western for a short period after this date until the service registrations could be placed in their own name. A more unusual purchase by Drawlane was Stagecoach's six-seater Cessna aircraft which had since its acquisition in 1988 had been used by the Scottish Group's directors when visiting the company's scattered outposts. Being somewhat spartan in its internal comforts, it had already been replaced a few weeks earlier

One of a large number of secondhand double deckers purchased by Ribble upon deregulation, former Southdown Park Royal-bodied Leyland Atlantean 1601 (PUF131M) hurries through Piccadilly, Manchester in the summer of 1989. As can be seen, it has had its front upper deck rebuilt in an unusual manner with a smaller side window to give the appearance of a thick corner pillar.

East Midland stretched MCW Metrorider 818 with Frontrunner North West and Ride a Roadrunner fleet names arrives at the Levenshulme, Manchester terminus of service 178 in September 1989 a few days before Frontrunner's operations were sold to the Drawlane group. (K.A.Jenkinson)

Leaving Stockport bus station on service 171 to Cheetham Hill on 3 October 1989 is former Grampian Alexander-bodied Leyland Atlantean 431 (KSA178P) which carried a paper sticker in its nearside windscreen indicating that it was operating on hire to North Western Road Car Co.Ltd. following the acquisition of Frontrunner's services by that Drawlane subsidiary. (K.A.Jenkinson)

by a larger, and more comfortable, Cessna 410-type 8-seat aircraft registered G-JEMS which, like its predecessor, was based at Scone airfield near Perth

In an attempt to tidy up its empire mainly for accountancy purposes, Stagecoach re-formed Hampshire Bus as Stagecoach South Ltd., placing both Hampshire Bus and United Counties under this new banner. Similarly, the Bee Line Buzz Company which had remained in Stagecoach ownership since the sale of its operations, vehicles and fleet name to Drawlane was re-named Stagecoach North West Limited and took over the activities of Cumberland Motor Services. Ribble will also ultimately be placed under the control of the latter although in none of the cases mentioned above was the trading name of the companies concerned altered.

Following the purchase in September of 23 new minibuses - 15 Reeve Burgess 25-seat Ivecos and 8 Reeve Burgess-bodied 31-seat Mercedes 811Ds - East Midland used these to replace conventional buses on several minor services although it was stated that the company did not have plans to make widescale use of small capacity vehicles throughout their territory. As if to highlight this, its five remaining ECW-bodied Bristol LH6Ls were transferred to Stagecoach's Tayside fleet for use in Perth and Dundee. Several other

vehicles were moved around the various subsidiaries during the month on both sides of the border. Hampshire Bus acquired one of Ribble's former Barrow Dodge S56 minibuses and took delivery of a further 5 new coach-seated Alexander-bodied Olympians while East Midland gained 7 new bus-seated Olympians with Alexander bodywork. East Midland also received a Plaxton Paramount-bodied Volvo B10M coach from United Counties to temporarily assist with a vehicle shortage in their coaching operations resulting from the disposal of two MCW Metroliner single deck coaches to Northern Travel Ltd. of Rotherham. Southdown borrowed a pair of Leyland Nationals and a Bristol VRT from Hampshire Bus and Cumberland loaned four of its tri-axle Talbot Pullman minibuses to Ribble for use on the services acquired from North Western. Cumberland also despatched one of its Leyland Olympian Megadekkas to Greater Manchester Buses who evaluated it in service from 4 to 11 September on a route which was also served by Frontrunner North West. While used on Greater Manchester's route 192, it became the subject of much local publicity when used as a getaway vehicle by a bank robber who had just stolen some £2,000 from Hazel Grove Trustee Savings Bank. The driver was unaware of the situation until the villain's shotgun fired accidentally in the upper saloon, blasting holes in the empty seats in front of him. As might have been expected, the local press carried a story relating to this incident, the headlines of which read 'Bank Bandit shoots up a Stagecoach'.

Acquired by Stagecoach from East Midland in October 1989, Bristol LH6L WVO855S spent only two months north of the border before being despatched to join the Hampshire Bus fleet. It is seen here splashing its way past Seagate Street bus station, Dundee on an extremely wet 27 October 1990 whilst working service 75. (K.A.Jenkinson)

Looking immaculate in its corporate livery, East Midland Reeve Burgess-bodied Mercedes minibus 726 (G826KWF) stands in the yard of Sutton Junction depot in August 1990. (P.French)

New to Barrow Borough Transport and later operated by Ribble, East Lancs-bodied Dodge S56 D460BEO then passed to Hampshire Bus with whom it is seen operating in corporate livery at Basingstoke bus station on 27 January 1990. (Ian Buck)

ACH141H, one of the ex.Cumberland Plaxton-bodied 40-seat Leyland Leopards transferred to Stagecoach in September 1989, despite having received corporate livery still showed its former owner's name on its rear glass plate as it awaited minor accident repairs at Swallow Coachworks former Highwayman premises at Errol on 27 October 1989. (K.A.Jenkinson)

In addition to receiving the five Bristol LH6Ls from East Midland, the Scottish operations gained a quartet of former Trent Plaxton coach-bodied 40-seat Leyland Leopards from Cumberland, three coach-seated Bristol VRTs from Hampshire Bus and permanently acquired the driver training Bristol FLF6G Lodekka which had been on loan from Hampshire Bus since June. More surprising however was the arrival on 25 September of 8 Ford Transit minibuses from Devon General which were hired for use on the expanded Perth Panther network which was due to be introduced in October. Even more surprising was the fact that these little buses all travelled from Exeter by train, thus taking the strain out of their 500 mile journey. One of the Magicbus Bristol FLF6Gs was taken out of reserve and returned to service at Perth while another bus of this type which had never been used since its acquisition in May 1987 was donated to a body promoting an anti-alcohol and drugs campaign in Glasgow.

An unexpected departure from Stagecoach's Scottish fleet was that of Bristol FLF6G Lodekka KPW487E which on 7 September departed for Malawi. Suitably adorned with signwriting bearing good wishes etc., it first visited Blantyre, Lanarkshire where it was loaded with medical supplies and gifts from the people of that Scottish town to the Queen Elizabeth Central Hospital in Blantyre, Malawi. Its journey was by sea to Durban in South Africa from where it travelled overland through Zimbabwe and Mozambique to arrive at it final destination on 3 November. Its cargo of gifts wa presented to a high-ranking official in Malawi's Ministry c Health by Ann Gloag at a special ceremony during the

following week and after this, the Lodekka then joined Stagecoach's Malawi fleet for eventual operational use. The connection between the two Blantyres dates back to David Livingstone, the explorer/missionary who was born in Blantyre, Scotland and eventually 'discovered' what is now Malawi. The official send-off from Scotland took place at the David Livingstone Memorial Centre in Blantyre which was partially funded by the Malawian Government.

Above : The poster affixed to the lower side panels of Stagecoach's Perth-based driver training Lodekkas offering PSV tuition in April 1991. (K.A.Jenkinson)

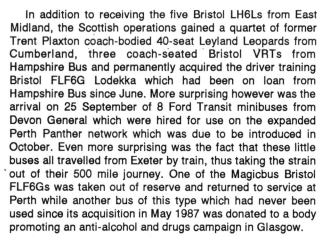

Left : Stagecoach's Bristol FLF6G driver training bus 073 (EMR288D) pictured here in all-yellow livery at Inveralmond depot, Perth on 6 April 1991 was acquired from Hampshire Bus in September 1989 after having spent the previous three months on loan to Stagecoach. (K.A.Jenkinson)

Letting the train take the strain, Devon General Ford Transit minibus C657FFJ together with a number of its sisters is seen here aboard a motorail train enroute from Exeter to Scotland on 2 October 1989 at the start of their period of loan to Perth Panther.

Never having been used by Stagecoach since its acquisition in May 1987, Bristol FLF 147YFM was in September 1989 donated to a charity for use in an anti alcohol and drugs campaign in the Strathclyde area.   (K.A.Jenkinson)

Back home, the Stagecoach Group were the subject of complaints to the Office of Fair Trading by both Lancaster City Council and Strathtay Scottish. Lancaster alleged that its operating arm was being put under undue pressure to contract its operations whilst Strathtay complained that the tactics adopted in the Tayside bus war were anti-competitive. Before the OFT could complete their investigations into these matters, Stagecoach's subsidiary, Ribble reached agreement with Lancaster City Transport to reorganise their services in Lancaster and Morecambe to provide a better service to passengers and both operators agreed to the interavailability of their tickets on routes shared between them. Lancaster also withdrew their longer-distance services to Preston and Blackpool and implemented these changes on 2 October.

Early in October, Brian Cox, who as well as being managing director of Hampshire Bus was also responsible for Stagecoach Group's operations in Scotland, relinquished the latter to take over the position as managing director of Southdown. His Scottish duties were then passed to Neil Renilson who was no stranger to the area, having himself been managing director of Strathtay Scottish until joining Stagecoach the previous month. Meanwhile, Ann Gloag, speaking at the BCC conference in Guernsey stated that she believed that Stagecoach's success was largely due to the excellent management team the company had assembled.

On the question of pay, she favoured individual negotiations at each company within the Stagecoach Group and indicated 'no deal' for any union pressure to return to the days of central negotiation. When asked if the company was wise in its policy of closing acquired central maintenance workshops, she pointed out that this decision allowed Stagecoach with its massive purchasing power to go to outside concerns and gain extremely good deals. Virtually every time central workshops had been inherited, these were found to be 'a

Standing on a cricket pitch in Blantyre, Malawi in November 1989 is recently-acquired ex.Stagecoach Bristol Lodekka KPW487E which was suitably lettered for its long journey from Scotland to Africa on which it carried gifts and medical supplies etc. (R.Bailey)

bastion of Union militancy, a paragon of inefficiency and a definite waste of resources'.

On a nostalgic note, as a result of the acquisition of Southdown and Ribble, Stagecoach had gained a further five 'historic' vehicles to add to their already preserved Bristol MW6G and ex.McLennans Leyland PS1. These, an open-top Leyland G-type and an open-top Leyland TD1 which had many years earlier been restored by Southdown and a pair of Leyland PLSC Lion single deckers and a more modern Leyland PD3 double decker refurbished by Ribble, were all maintained to PSV standards and were available for use on special occasions. Painted in the traditional liveries of their former owners, they were regarded by their new masters as valuable assets and as such, had the prospect of a healthy future.

One of the preserved buses inherited with the Ribble fleet was this 1927 Leyland PLSC1 Lion which although looking completely authentic, carries a replica body built in Ribble's workshops in 1981. Finished in the company's original livery, CK3825 is restored to full PSV standards and in addition to being used to attend vintage vehicle events, it is available for special private hire and other duties.   (K.A.Jenkinson)

*Acquired by Ribble from Blackburn Transport in 1986 in conventional closed-top form, East Lancs-bodied Leyland Atlantean 1622 (JFR394N) was later converted to open-top configuration and is seen here on Morecambe promenade on service 421 in 1988 in white, grey & red livery.
(K.A.Jenkinson)*

*Included in the acquisition of Ribble Motor Services was that company's three preserved buses - two Leyland PLSC Lions and a Metro Cammell-bodied Leyland PD3/5. The latter, TCK841 which wears Ribble's pre-NBC livery of crimson & cream, is occasionally used in normal service and is seen here on Morecambe promenade working a duty on the 421 to Heysham Village on 30 June 1988.
(K.A.Jenkinson)*

Opposite page :

Left column, top to bottom :

*On hire to Bee Line Buzz on 3 October 1989 immediately after the sale of Frontrunner North West's operations to the Drawlane group. East Midland Leyland National 534 (WNO562L) with Frontrunner fleet names leaves Stockport bus station on the 363 route to Glossop.
(K.A.Jenkinson)*

*Former Portsmouth CityBus Alexander-bodied Atlantean 343 received a non-standard livery of white with three red bands & chevrons after its acquisition by the Stagecoach group. Seen here in its home city on 19 January 1991, it also carried its new owner's Portsmouth fleet names.
(MG Photographic)*

*Also acquired with Portsmouth CityBus was the Red Admiral minibus operation in the city. Here, Robin Hood-bodied Iveco E969LPX is seen still in its original livery at Portsea on 3 March 1990.
(Ian Buck)*

1018 (WVT618), one of Southdown's Plaxton Paramount-bodied Leyland Tigers in National Express livery leaves Fareham on the 075 service from Portsmouth to London in 1990.   (F.W.York)

Right column, top to bottom :

Leaving East Midland's Clowne depot in November 1990, Plaxton-bodied Bedford YMT driver training bus LPT872T still wears the old Rainworth Travel livery of white & dark blue.   (K.A.Jenkinson)

About to enter Poole depot after working an X72 journey from Andover is Hampshire Bus Bristol VRT 3366 (RJT157R), still painted in the pre-Stagecoach era livery of red, white & blue.   (A.Gilmour)

*Ribble at first operated its former Frontrunner South East ex.Greater Manchester Atlanteans in Frontrunner's two-tone green & cream livery before eventually repainting them into Stagecoach corporate colours. One such bus, 1684 (LJA641P), complete with red Ribble fleet names, stands in Blackburn bus station on 25 October 1989.
(K.A.Jenkinson)*

Although by the time this photograph was taken, Cedarbus of Worthing MCW Metrorider F563HPP had passed to Southdown, it still wore its original owner's livery as it operated service C3 to Durrington in November 1989.

MOVING TO NEW HOMES

Having continued to use the office and depot premises at Walnut Grove, Perth since its sale to National Express on 4 August, Stagecoach Holdings after much searching found new accommodation in Charlotte Street, Perth towards the end of August in Charlotte House, a building previously occupied by Blair Insurance Services (Stagecoach's insurance claims handling firm). Being closer to the city centre than Walnut Grove, this became the Group's new headquarters and also incorporated a travel office within its spacious reception area. To allow the move from Walnut Grove to be completed, new depot premises were found on the Inveralmond Industrial Estate on the northern fringe of the city and these were brought into use on 21 October. This 'new' depot was in reality, an area of open land upon which the only building was a portacabin. The ex.Cumberland Bristol VRT which, still wearing its NBC poppy red livery and sporting Cumberland advertising posters had been withdrawn from service a couple of weeks earlier was put to use as a store room whilst a withdrawn former Kelvin Leopard single decker was turned into a uniform store with a B & Q garden shed completing the buildings inventory as the cleaners facilities ! As the site contained no undercover facilities for vehicle maintenance, a small unit was leased nearby on the Industrial Estate at which all minibus maintenance was handled while conventional-size vehicles were cared for by Stagecoach's Spittalfield depot.

In Perth, the Panther network was revised on 9 October when, continuing the pressure on Strathtay Scottish, their services became identical to those run by Strathtay and were timed to run four or five minutes ahead of the state-controlled company. This increased the number of Panther vehicles required in Perth and use was made of the hired 16-seat Devon General Ford Transits of which there were now 20, the remaining 12 having arrived by train on 2 October. These still retained their original owner's maroon & cream livery - albeit with their Bay Line fleet names removed and although some gained Magicbus legal lettering, no other

Still in NBC poppy red livery and fitted with Cumberland advertising posters, recently-withdrawn Bristol VRT HHH 273N is seen here at Stagecoach's new Inveralmond, Perth depot on 27 October 1989 in use as a store room. (S.K.Jenkinson)

visible identification as to their operator was carried, adding yet further confusion to the Perth bus scene where four totally separate operators appeared to be running to the uninformed passenger (maroon & cream Transits; Panthers in Stagecoach corporate colours; Strathtay in blue & orange and claret-liveried Perth City Transport Routemasters !). To further bolster the Perth fleet, another 8 new Iveco minibuses were taken into stock, all of which carried full Stagecoach livery and were adorned with Panther Cub logos.

Outside Scotland, Ribble recast several of its services in Preston on 16 October after reaching some territorial

In service in Perth on 27 October 1989 on city service 2 was hired Devon General Ford Transit C677FFJ which, although retaining its rightful owner's maroon & cream livery was given Magicbus (Scotland) Ltd. legal lettering. (S.A.JenKinson)

Left : Charlotte House, Perth, Stagecoach Holdings new headquarters and travel office. (K.A.Jenkinson)

agreement with Preston Borough Transport and withdrew all its Zippy minibus routes north of the river Ribble. Two weeks earlier, on 2 October, Ribble had closed its small depot at Garstang, transferring its allocation to Preston and Lancaster. Further south, East Midland successfully gained a number of South Yorkshire PTE tenders in the Doncaster area, partly at the expense of Yorkshire Traction. These new services were branded 'Dearne Valley' whilst the new coach-seated Olympians were introduced onto a revised Sheffield - Nottingham express service. In Sussex, Eastbourne's journeys on Top Line's route 98 (Eastbourne - Hastings) passed to Southdown on 29 October.

The now customary movement of vehicles between Stagecoach's various subsidiaries continued unabated and to supplement the new Portsmouth fleet, two Dormobile-bodied 16-seat Freight Rover Sherpa minibuses were transferred from Hampshire Bus. Ribble gained 5 Bristol VRTs from East Midland and acquired the chassis of a former Cumberland 1934 Leyland Lion LT5A from a group of Yorkshire enthusiasts, adding this to its 'preserved' fleet for future restoration while the four tri-axle Talbot Pullmans were returned to Cumberland following their use at Blackburn. Southdown acquired a pair of Bristol VRTs from United Counties for spares and gained three stretched MCW Metroriders from East Midland who in turn loaned one of its ex.Magicbus Routemasters to South Yorkshire independent, Rotherham & District. More new coach-seated Alexander-bodied Leyland Olympians were taken into stock with 4 being allocated to United Counties and 10 to Ribble who placed them in service on their 140/2 (Preston/Blackpool - Morecambe) and 167/8 (Accrington - Blackpool) routes. United Counties also received 6 new Iveco minibuses. In Scotland, an ex.Northern General Routemaster of Magicbus was withdrawn following accident damage while a former London example, which had been held in reserve since April, was sold to a dealer. Transferred from Cumberland to Magicbus was a Duple-bodied Volvo B58 coach which had previously operated from Perth between 1986 and 1988, and upon its arrival at Glasgow, Leyland National 206 became the first of its type to be withdrawn north of the border. Finally, the remains of the former Cotters Van Hool-bodied Volvo UHV59, were cut up at Spittalfield where it had reclined since being severely damaged by fire in April 1988.

Stagecoach's corporate identity was now gaining strength at a rapid rate and in addition to the white, orange, blue & red livery being applied upon repaint to all the vehicles operated by its subsidiaries, the group's identity was being extended to all publicity material and timetable leaflets etc. The new logo devised for Stagecoach Holdings Ltd. based on the geograhical outline of Great Britain started to appear on much of the group's printed matter, including that of its subsidiaries, and also began to be applied to vehicles repainted into the group's corporate livery (in addition to the particular operating company's fleet name), leaving no doubt as to their parentage.

STAGECOACH HOLDINGS Ltd

Above : Cumberland 560 (XNE884L), an ex.Kirkpatricks Plaxton-bodied Leyland Leopard maintained in its former owner's livery, passes Workington bus station whilst working a local service on 11 April 1989.   (A.Gilmour)

Opposite page :

Left column, top to bottom :

2523, one of Gray Coach Lines MCI 102A3-type three-axle coaches of 1986 vintage typifies Stagecoach's Canadian fleet. It is seen here at Lakeside maintenance depot, Toronto in April 1991 whilst being prepared for its next duty. (Stagecoach)

One of the ex.Kowloon Motor Bus Co. Metsec-bodied Daimler CVG6 buses supplied by Speedybus Enterprises for operation in the Peoples' Republic of China is seen here in service on 28 December 1990 after being rebuilt with its entrance doors positioned on the offside.   (C.Lau)

Although acquired by Cumberland with the fleet of W.A.Palmer, Carlisle Willowbrook-bodied Ford R192 FTC850J was not operated by its new owner and was instead placed in store.   (K.A.Jenkinson)

Out of use at Stagecoach's Spittalfield depot in March 1990, Bristol FLF6G Lodekka 077 (GRX132D) still carried the old style Magicbus fleet name on its somewhat faded livery. (K.A.Jenkinson)

Right column, top to bottom :

Wearing the pre-Stagecoach Cityline two-tone blue livery of Stagecoach Malawi, Leyland Victory Mk.2 354 of 1985 vintage is pictured here in a Blantyre suburb in October 1989.   (R.Bailey)

Several preserved buses are included in Stagecoach's combined fleet one of which is this 1929 open-top Leyland TD1 of Southdown in whose original livery it is painted.   (P.T.Stokes)

East Midland have adopted the Midland Travel fleet name for their coaching operations. Carrying its new Midland Travel Coachstyle fleet name is Plaxton Paramount 3500-bodied Leyland Tiger 56 (NIB4887, originally B56DKW) seen at Harrogate on an excursion in June 1990.   (K.A.Jenkinson)

Upon its arrival in Scotland in the autumn of 1990, former Southdown convertible open-top Bristol VRT UWV608S was, in closed top form, quickly pressed into service at Perth still wearing its previous owner's livery. Sporting both Southdown fleet number 608 and Stagecoach number 106 on its front panel, it was also adorned with Stagecoach fleet name vinyls.   (K.A.Jenkinson)

Below : Also seen operating a Workington town service on 11 April 1989 was Cumberland 32, a Reeve Burgess-bodied Dodge S56 in its owner's dark red & sandstone livery with a brown skirt on which was displayed the CMS Minibus fleet name. (A.Gilmour)

Below : Wearing Ribble's attractive grey, white, red & black dual purpose livery, Duple-bodied Leyland Leopard 1099 (KRN99T) rests at Blackpool before starting its return journey to Liverpool on the 761 service.   (K.A.Jenkinson)

FURTHER EXPANSION IN THE SOUTH

Undoubtedly, the major news of October was the purchase on the 20th of the month of Portsmouth Citybus, a former municipal undertaking in which Southampton City Transport owned a 75% share and StartRight (the Portsmouth Citybus workforce) held the remaining 25%. An ailing company, Citybus together with its Red Admiral minibus operation had for some considerable time been facing ever-increasing competition from both Southdown and People's Provincial and it was clearly evident that a great deal of reorganisation and planning would be required in order to improve its trading position. Immediately made a subsidiary of Southdown and placed under the direction of Brian Cox, it was obvious that a rationalisation of the services of both companies would be needed to eliminate wastage and put the Portsmouth company onto a firm footing. Although no immediate changes were made and the inherited Citybus fleet which consisted mainly of Leyland Atlanteans, Leyland Nationals and Iveco minibuses continued to be operated in their ivory & crimson livery, it was only a matter of days before the first of these was repainted into Stagecoach corporate colours to provide an early taste of what was inevitably to come.

Within weeks of taking over Portsmouth Citybus, it was announced early in November that as part of its rationalisation plans, all the bus services in the city would ultimately be placed under the Southdown Portsmouth banner and would be centred on the Citybus depot at Eastney which had been secured on a three-year lease from the city council. This would allow Southdown's Hilsea depot to be closed and sold for redevelopment and looking to the longer term, negotiations were already taking place in an attempt to extend the lease on the Eastney premises. As part of the deal struck with Southampton City Transport during the purchase of Citybus, it was agreed to transfer two Hampshire Bus services - the half-hourly stopping inter-urban 47 between Winchester and Southampton and Southdown's share of the joint Southampton - Portsmouth express service of which Southampton CityBus already had part - to the council-owned company early in 1990.

With the dust hardly having settled on the south coast, Stagecoach, through its Magicbus subsidiary, acquired yet another company, this being in north-west Scotland, almost 600 miles from Portsmouth. Inverness Traction, the minibus company rescued by Alexander (North East) after it was set to close down in April 1989, was purchased on 14 November as its masters went into receivership. With the Inverness business came a number of town services along with 22 Freight Rover Sherpa minibuses and 6 Leyland Leopards, two of which were ex. Stagecoach vehicles acquired only four months earlier. Ironically, the Inverness operation was placed under the control of Neil Renilson who, whilst

Above : Still painted in the red & black livery of Red Admiral. Robin Hood-bodied Iveco 49.10 E959LPX is seen in Commercial Road, Portsmouth on 22 November 1989 after being acquired by the Stagecoach group. (A.G.Izatt)

Below : Painted in an all-white livery and given Red Admiral fleet names, 61 (D961WJH) was one of a pair of Dormobile-bodied Freight Rover Sherpas acquired with the Portsmouth fleet in 1989. It is seen here in Commercial Road, Portsmouth on its way to Eastney on 22 November 1989. (A.G.Izatt)

Portsmouth CityBus Alexander-bodied Leyland Atlantean 292, complete with luggage trailer, helps with the move from Hilsea (East) to Eastney depot on the bus's and depot's last day of operation on 20 January 1990. (A.G.Izatt)

managing director of Strathtay Scottish hsd sent buses free of charge to SBG subsidiary, Highland, to help them attack Inverness Traction soon after its formation and now had to repair the damage he had helped to cause ! Apart from the 6 Leopards which were owned, all of the Inverness Traction vehicles were leased, and Stagecoach were keen to return these to their leasing companies and replace them with Group-owned buses as soon as possible. Stagecoach took over at midnight on 11 November and by 3.00am on 12 November had transferred 3 vehicles from Perth to Inverness to help meet the morning peak requirements on the first day

D28PVS, one of Inverness Traction's leased Dormobile-bodied Freight Rover Sherpa minibuses, is seen here in front of Inverness Library soon after Traction's acquisition by Stagecoach in November 1989. One of the first to be withdrawn from service, it last operated in January 1990.

of operation under Stagecoach ownership. Before many days had elapsed, Cumberland despatched eight of its tri-axle Talbot Pullman minibuses to Stagecoach's Spittalfield premises for onward transfer to Inverness, these being joined early in December by the remaining two vehicles of this same batch. Similarly, Magicbus transferred two of its coaches - a Leyland Leopard and a Volvo - to Inverness during November in order to further supplement the Traction fleet.

Having gained the Strathclyde PTE tender to provide the Sunday operation on a service in the Glasgow area running from Clydebank to Parkhall, Magicbus once again turned their attention towards Tayside where, on 27 November, it started a new service - numbered 57 - between Dundee and Blairgowrie which copied that operated by Strathtay using the same number. To attract passengers to this new service, adverts were inserted in the local press which, in addition to showing the time table and fares, also included two free travel vouchers which could be used by passengers on the new 57 service up to and including 9 December. Since the Perth and Dundee bus wars had started some five months earlier, the revision of services and introduction of competitive routes by both Magicbus and Strathtay Scottish had become almost a weekly occurrence and as a result of Stagecoach Holdings' policy of undercutting fares, Strathtay had been forced to reduce many of their charges by up to 50% with 60p fares being halved to 30p. Although neither operator could claim to be making a substantial profit from these operations, the travelling public were obviously gaining great benefit from the conflict, enjoying lower fares and a much higher service frequency than they had previously experienced.

In Lancashire, peace returned to Blackburn on 20

November following an agreement reached between Ribble and Blackburn Transport as to their service networks in and around the town and following lengthy discussions, much of the previous wasteful competition was eliminated. Prior to this, on 13 November, East Midland introduced some of its 15 recently-delivered Ivecos and 8 Mercedes 811D minibuses into the Worksop and Bassetlaw areas where most of the services had been recast with significant economies being achieved.

November proved to be a comparatively quiet month as far

One of the Alexander-bodied Leyland Leopards acquired from Inverness Traction, still in light grey livery, stands withdrawn at Stagecoach's Spittalfield depot in March 1990 before being despatched to Cumberland Motor Services for use as a driver training vehicle.   (K.A.Jenkinson)

as inter-fleet vehicle transfers were concerned with fewer movements between companies taking place than had become customary. In addition to the previously mentioned departures to Inverness, Stagecoach's five short-lived ex. East Midland Bristol LH6Ls were transferred to Hampshire Bus after giving less than eight weeks service north of the border. A further two Perth Panther Leyland Nationals were delicenced and placed in the reserve fleet at Spittalfield, their duties having passed to minibuses whilst from East Midland, Stagecoach received a trio of Plaxton-bodied, coach-seated Leyland Leopards. More unusually however, two preserved double deckers - a Leyland PD2/24 and a Daimler CVD6-30 - both of which carried Alexander bodywork and had been delivered new to Glasgow Corporation in 1958 were hired from a Scottish enthusiast in November. Looking superb in their original owner's orange, green & cream livery, these were placed in service on Magicbus's 19 service from Glasgow to Easterhouse running alongside ex.London Routemasters. and remained on these duties until a few days after Christmas. Also loaned from this same enthusiast was a preserved ex.Strathtay Scottish AEC Matador recovery wagon which was allocated to Spittalfield where it had the word 'NOT' inserted in front of its Strathtay Scottish fleet name. Having regained its cherished registration numbers 2412SC, 4585SC, 5142SC and 9492SC from Caledonian Express following their removal from the Neoplans sold to that company in August, Stagecoach used these to disguise the age of the four former Trent Leopards which had been acquired from Cumberland in September. Also re-registered at this same time was an ex. Highwayman Volvo which received 449CLT from one of Magicbus' ex. London Routemasters.

Other vehicle news saw the loan of one of Southdown's coach-seated Leyland Leopards to Portsmouth Citybus, and the return to Cumberland of two of their minibuses off loan from United Counties whilst East Midland hired one of their

Loaned from a preservationist for use as Stagecoach's Spittalfield towing wagon, former Strathtay Scottish AEC Matador FYS8 retained its previous owner's colours but had 'NOT' inserted in front of its Strathtay fleet name. (K.A.Jenkinson)

Gamull Lane into its own operations and thus, in addition to eliminating competition, was able to make a saving on vehicle mileage.

Within five days, Stagecoach had added yet another company to its growing empire with the purchase by its Cumberland subsidiary on the first day of December of Carlisle-based independent, W.A.Palmer. This gave the Group their first cross-boder stage carriage services and an additional 8 vehicles, although all of these which were of Ford and Bedford manufacture, were immediately delicenced

Leyland Nationals to Sheffield-based independent, Yorkshire Terrier from mid-November to early December. In Carlisle, Cumberland Atlantean 1474 was de-roofed in a low bridge accident at Upperby on 12 November, causing its premature withdrawal from service while East Midland were by now introducing their five ex.Magicbus Routemasters in service in Mansfield. In the following months, instead of being repainted into the Group's corporate colours, some of these were treated individually with one receiving the old East Midland livery of brown, biscuit & cream; one gaining the erstwhile Mansfield District Tramways colours of green, cream & silver and the others being finished in a predominantly white advertising livery.

Before the month ended, Stagecoach Holdings whose expansion programme ground on relentlessly, purchased the stage carriage operations and vehicles of Mercers of Longridge, near Preston on 26 November, adding this to their Ribble portfolio. An old-established family run coaching firm, Mercers had only entered the stage carriage field in October 1986 upon the implementation of deregulation, but since that date had, in addition to registering a number of commercially operated services, gained several contracts under tender from Lancashire County Council. Although its 20-strong bus fleet - 10 Fleetline double deckers; 3 Leyland Nationals; 3 Leyland Leopards and 4 Freight Rover Sherpa minibuses - passed to Ribble, it was expected that none of these would be retained for more than a few weeks and that several would not turn a wheel with their new owner. Mercer's coaching activities and premises at Grimsargh were not included in the deal and indeed the independent intended to expand this side of its business and in addition set up an engineering unit specialising in the rebuilding and reconditioning of engines etc. Ribble almost immediately integrated Mercers' services to Longridge, Leyland and

Originating from London Transport, Mercers' Daimler Fleetline OJD222R is seen here outside its owner's depot a few weeks before the company's stage carriage operations were sold to Ribble. (T.W.W.Knowles)

Below left : Seen at the Clipstone terminus of route 16 in October 1990 is East Midland Routemaster NSG636A (formerly 164CLT) which has been beautifully painted in the company's old biscuit, brown & cream livery. (K.A.Jenkinson)

Below : Sporting a predominantly white livery with Mansfield & District fleet names, ex.Magicbus Routemaster WTS418A (originally WLT909) prepares to leave Clipstone on its return to Mansfield on route 16 in October 1990. (K.A.Jenkinson)

Looking smart in United Counties pre-Stagecoach livery of dark green, orange, yellow & cream at Luton bus station is KRU852W, a Bristol VRT acquired from Hampshire Bus. (T.G.Walker)

Palmer of Carlisle's Duple-bodied Ford R1114 SCK331L is seen here at Morecambe in 1989 whilst working a private hire the border city. Although acquired by Cumberland with Palmer's operations, this coach was never operated by its new owners. (T.W.W.Knowles)

and placed in store at Cumberland's Carlisle depot and were never operated by their new owner. Palmer worked a total of seven local and rural routes, the main one of which ran from Carlisle to Gretna Green and Longtown, and all of these were continued by Cumberland. No property was included in the deal.

Meanwhile, the ongoing battle in Perth continued without respite and following an announcement by Strathtay Scottish that it was to further increase its frequency on its routes to North Muirton, Stagecoach replied by introducing Sunday services to the city on 3 December, these competing directly with those operated by Strathtay with a regional subsidy, Following this move, the Regional Council promptly withdrew Strathtay's subsidy ! An even greater use was made of the Group's Panther Cub minibus fleet, although Leyland Nationals continued to appear on Perth's more heavily-loaded city services, and following the attacks and counter attacks, the residents of Muirton who at the start of the bus was enjoyed a 15-minute service frequency, unbelievingly found they had a timetabled bus every two minutes with duplicates pushing the actual frequency up to every 60/90 seconds. Further north, Inverness Traction reintroduced two services which it had abandoned prior to its takeover by Stagecoach Holdings and began several new routes in an attempt to regain its former status in the town, competing vigourously with its rival, Highland Scottish.

East Midland was in the meantime facing disruption of its services when the National Union of Railwaymen imposed an overtime ban following the dismissal of a fitter. In an attempt to keep the services running normally during this troubled period, East Midland's managing director, George Watson, quickly assembled a troubleshooting squad by importing

relief drivers from other Stagecoach subsidiaries, including a bus load from Scotland comprising volunteers from all the Scottish depots. For a couple of weeks, the Mansfield town services were then run by a combination of Inverness Traction inspectors and Perth Panther and Magicbus drivers, giving Highland and Strathtay Scottish a brief respite as all duplication was withdrawn to free drivers to send to East Midland. In addition to climbing behind the wheel himself, George Watson was joined by Brian Souter who also took on a driver's role and drove several journeys on the Chesterfield - Nottingham service. Accommodation for the 'imported' crews was provided by the company in local hotels, motels and guest houses during their period 'away from home'. As a result of this swift response, the NUR subsequently dropped its action and normality once again returned as a new era of industrial relations began in the company.

With effect from 1 December, Ribble underwent a managerial restructuring when Brian Souter, who previously controlled the company directly, appointed Barry Hinkley as managing director, a post which he already held with Cumberland and United Counties. To give him additional time for his new duties at Ribble, Tony Cox was appointed general manager at United Counties and Tim Archer expanded his role as Ribble's commercial director.

United Counties introduced a new minibus service in Daventry using a trio of Phoenix-bodied 25-seat Iveco 49.10s in corporate livery with the addition of Street Shuttle fleet names. The new service, which was registered commercially, was built around some school contracts obtained by United Counties in September and from the outset, was hailed as a great success.

East Midland's open-top Bristol VRT 175 was a long way from home when caught by the camera at Basingstoke bus station on 19 August 1989 whilst being used in connection with Stagecoach's Basingstoke rally and open day. (Ian Buck)

WINNERS AT THE BATTLE OF HASTINGS

Following much talk and speculation during the previous months of the possible sale by Stagecoach of Hastings Top Line Buses to Milton Keynes City Bus who themselves were attempting to take over Hastings & District Transport Co., the Perth-based company's Southdown subsidiary, on 8 December, suddenly stepped in and purchased the Formia Group, owners of Hastings & District Transport, Hastings Coaches, Eastbourne & District Transport and Cinque Ports Travel. Included in this deal was Hastings & District's fleet which comprised Leyland Nationals, Leyland Atlanteans, Bristol VRTs, Bristol REs, Leyland Leopard and Tiger coaches and a large number of Mercedes L608D minibuses and depots at Rye and Silverhill (St.Leonards on Sea). Two liveries were in use at the time of the takeover, one being ivory and maroon, the other, blue, yellow & cream.

The first stage of Portsmouth Citybus's forthcoming merger with Southdown was heralded on 4 December by the introduction of tickets which were interchangeable between the two companies. Two weeks later, on 16 December, Top Line, to bring them into line with their new Hastings & District neighbour, withdrew their 'return fare for the price of a single journey' offer and at the same time, child fares ceased to be available before 9.00am and between 3.30pm and 5.30pm Monday to Friday on service 98 west of Sidley. Top Line also lost its last remaining double deckers during the month when Atlanteans 414/5 (YJK933/2V) were transferred to

Portsmouth Citybus who also acquired 6 former Frontrunner North West Alexander-bodied Atlanteans from East Midland. These entered service on the south coast still wearing their previous owner's two-tone green & cream livery and fleet names.

During December, Hampshire Bus lost one of its series 3 Bristol VRTs when, on the night of the 7th, 323 was destroyed by fire at Andover depot. Believed to have been caused by an electrical fault on this vehicle, the severity of the blaze resulted in the depot roof also been damaged and had it not been for the bravery of staff who moved numerous vehicles out of the depot, the consequences would have undoubtedly been much more serious. To replace 323 and thus maintain Andover's vehicle requirements, series 2 Bristol VRT 315 was given a new lease of life and was returned to service after being withdrawn some nine months earlier. Another fire victim was United Counties Robin Hood-bodied Iveco minibus 21, this being replaced by a new Phoenix-bodied Iveco diverted from Southdown. Hampshire Bus also acquired 2 Leyland Leopards from United Counties while Cumberland gained a pair of Leyland Nationals from Ribble and evaluated the DiPTAC-modified South Wales Leyland National 2 in service at Carlisle for three weeks from 11 December.

Magicbus's three-axle Olympian Megadekka, which normally saw use in Glasgow and its surrounds, was

Above : Mercedes 608D minibus GCD220V was used for driver training purposes by Hastings & District at whose Silverhill depot it is seen here on 21 April 1990.   (A.G.Izatt)

Above left : In its blue, cream & yellow livery, Hastings & District full-height ECW-bodied Bristol VRT 535 passes through its home town on 6 March 1990.   (Ian Buck)

Still painted in Hastings & District cream and crimson 'Arrow' livery, Leyland National 310 is seen here on the 513 service to Lydd. (T.W.W.Knowles)

transferred to Perth for the duration of the Christmas school holidays and was widely used on a number of services during its brief stay giving the residents of some Perth estates the choice of travelling on the largest and smallest buses in Scotland on the same route (16-seat Devon General Ford Transits followed by the 110-seat Megadekka). The Olympian's replacement in Glasgow was a preserved former Blackpool Transport Leyland PD3A/1 with open rear platform MCW bodywork which was hired for a short period during December and early January 1990. Unlike the two preserved ex. Glasgow Corporation buses which were used regularly in service, the Blackpool double decker saw only occasional use. The first of Inverness Traction's minibuses were repossessed before Stagecoach took control of the company and left in penny numbers on a weekly basis thereafter. At the end of December, another of Stagecoach's Leyland Nationals was withdrawn and placed in store whilst three buses of this type left Perth to join the Cumberland Motor Services fleet, two having originated from this source six months earlier. Also delicenced and placed in store was Stagecoach's convertible open-top Bristol FS6G Lodekka.

Across the water in Malawi, having found its double deckers to be a great success, Stagecoach, via Hong Kong-based Speedybus, acquired a further five ex.Kowloon Daimler CVG6s together with five Duple bodied Albion EVK55CL-type coaches from this same source. One of the Albions never entered service in its new home however, and was instead cannibalised for spares. By now, double deck operation had resulted in over 60% growth in patronage, with a negligable increase in the number of kilometers operated, and thus led to their operation being extended to several other services in the Blantyre area including the Blantyre - Limbe via Soche corridor and routes to Chiradzulu, Mirale and Lunzu. Meanwhile, the former Stagecoach Bristol Lodekka which had arrived on 3 November still at this time rested in the company's Chichiri workshops at Blantyre, having not yet been placed in passenger service while the ex. United Counties Leyland Tiger was used mainly on the Coachline service from Blantyre to Lilongwe. During the period since Stagecoach had gained its controlling interest in the Malawi company, a large number of its services had been revised and several of those discontinued during the previous couple of years were reinstated. Some of the 'country' routes operated to different timetables during the wet and dry seasons and two International Express services were introduced, one operating from Lilongwe to Lusaka in Zambia, the other from Lilongwe to Harare. That to Lusaka was operated jointly by Stagecoach and UBZ of Zambia and had a journey time of 13 hours (including a 90 minute break at the Mwami border point) and operated outward from Lilongwe on Sundays and Wednesdays, returning on Tuesdays and Thursdays. An unusual feature of the daily 113 service between Blantyre and Lilongwe is that two of the 8 hour 30 minute journeys in each direction are operated by Leyland Victory Mk.2 buses hauling freight trailers. A total of 73 buses of this type, plus 3 Victory Mk.1s are fitted with bodywork incorporating a rear freight compartment for use on specified services and of these, 13 are additionally equipped with towing hooks to enable them to haul freight trailers.

ENTERING A NEW DECADE

Compared with the events of the previous year, the new decade opened quietly, although this proved to be only a brief respite before the wheels of change were put into motion yet again. On 2 January, Hastings & District ceased the practice of outstationing one of its Eastbourne & District minibuses at Pevensey and began to re-number some of its vehicles so as not to duplicate other Southdown group buses and coaches. Five days later, a reorganisation of Hastings & District routes was undertaken and on 14 January, Top Line moved from its Farrants Yard premises into Hastings & District's Silverhill depot where space was made by the removal of a number of delicensed and stored vehicles to the Coach Station and Bulverhythe. Despite having moved from Farrants Yard, a shed was retained on this site where more withdrawn vehicles were placed. The phased integration of Top Line with Hastings & District had now begun and on the following day Top Line's fares were brought into line with those charged on parallel Hastings & District services and full interavailability of both companies' tickets was introduced. This interavailability was also extended to Bexhill Bus Company's route 10 and Southdown's 98 service along Bexhill Road.

during the above weekend and within days the new Southdown Portsmouth fleet name had begun to appear on several members of the fleet painted in Stagecoach's corporate livery. Those still sporting their former operator's colours retained their Citybus names however and it was to be some considerable time before this disappeared completely. The opportunity was taken to rationalise the Group's services in Portsmouth where several had previously been duplicated by both operators, and as a result of this, 49 of Citybus's L and N-registered Atlanteans were able to be withdrawn. Meanwhile, along the coast, Cedar Travel, who had sold their stage carriage operations to Southdown in September 1989, cheekily re-entered this field with a new cross town route in Worthing and another to Midhurst.

East Midland Duple Laser-bodied Leyland Tiger 46 (NIB5455, originally A46YAK) in Midland Travel Coachstyle livery approaches Mansfield bus station in September 1990 enroute to Blackpool. (P.T.Stokes)

Above : In March 1990, Hastings & District full-height Bristol VRT 523 still wore its owner's now obsolete 'Arrow' livery of cream & crimson. (Ian Buck)

Below : Looking resplendent in Stagecoach group corporate livery and carrying Portsmouth fleet names, former Citybus Alexander-bodied Atlantean 322, seen here on 19 January 1990, had an electronic route number indicator fitted to the nearside of its front destination screen.   (A.G.Izatt)

Along the coast, Portsmouth Citybus was fully merged with Southdown on the night of 20/21 January and as a result, Southdown's Hilsea depot was closed and all its operations transferred to the former Citybus depot at Eastney. All the former Citybus vehicles received Southdown legal lettering

A trio of Portsmouth Citybus Alexander-bodied Atlanteans rest in Eastney depot on 20 January 1990. 334 has already gained Stagecoach-group corporate livery whilst 338 and 283 both still retain Citybus colours. (A.G.Izatt)

Confusion in Portsmouth on 4 January 1990.. Former East Midland Leyland National HCA976N, still in its former owner's livery complete with fleet names already carried its new Hampshire Bus fleet number 738 but was on hire to Southdown. Caught by the camera outside Hilsea depot, it was showing route 345 Fareham on its destination screen. (A.G.Izatt)

Hampshire Bus moved its Botley outstation to the yard of Hills Transport on 22 January while on that same day, Stagecoach fired new shots at Strathtay Scottish by extending its 74 service from Carnoustie to Arbroath and altering the 75 to run via Broomhill Drive and Ashludie Hospital. Together, these routes now provided a 10 minute frequency between Dundee and Monifieth and provided an even greater challenge to Strathtay on their lucrative Tayway services bearing these same numbers.

Returning to the south coast, the severe gales which lashed the area on 25 January caused Hastings & District 522 to be blown off the road at Jury's Gap and 526 to be swept through a fence into a field at East Guldeford. Although 522 was able to be recovered - with extreme difficulty - that same evening, it was not until the following day that the surprisingly undamaged 526 was rescued. As a result of these weather conditions, all the services using Hastings sea front were diverted via White Rock Gardens

In full Top Line yellow & black livery but now carrying a Hastings fleet name above its front destination box, ex.Eastbourne East Lancs-bodied Leyland Atlantean 525 passes through Hastings on 26 May 1990. (D.W.Rhodes)

Repainted into Stagecoach group corporate colours and wearing a Portsmouth fleet name, former Portsmouth CityBus Leyland National 2 CPO98W prepares to leave Fareham on its way to Southsea on service 65 in the autumn of 1990. (F.W.York)

Having been returned to Cumberland after its use by Inverness Traction, and painted in Traction's grey livery, Talbot Pullman tri-axle minibus D78RVM is seen here in store at Hindpool Road depot, Barrow in Furness on 10 October 1990 awaiting a decision on its future. (D.J.Smithies)

Standing inside Magicbus's Warroch Street, Glasgow depot on 24 February 1990, much-travelled NCME-bodied Atlantean 1668 (KBU913P) still carried Ribble fleetnames. It was withdrawn by Magicbus in March 1990 and returned to Ribble three months later. (K.A.Jenkinson)

Midland, on the final day of the month, loaned four of its MCW Metrorider minibuses to London Buses for driver training purposes. Two of these were allocated to London Buses' Hounslow garage, the other pair being used at Fulwell and it was not until March that these returned to their rightful owner. Overseas, 10 more ex.Kowloon Daimler CVG6 double deckers had been added to the Malawi fleet, bringing the total of this type to 35.

By the start of 1990, Stagecoach's corporate livery was being applied to the vehicles of almost all the group's subsidiaries at an ever increasing rate, although it must be said that none had yet completed this task and each individual company still had a number of vehicles in pre-Stagecoach colours. Top Line Leyland National 27, which received its corporate identity in January was sprayed white by Eastbourne Buses and had its stripes added by Southdown. Upon completion, it was returned to service without fleet names, highlighting the speculation that Top Line was set to disappear in the not too distant future.

and other roads and double deckers were removed from all services for a time. Similar problems were experienced along the whole of the south coast and in the Portsmouth area, traffic locked solid due to most roads being closed. It was not only the south of England that suffered as these gales swept across most of Britain and on 25 January, United Counties Leyland National 544 was crushed by a falling tree, resulting in its early demise.

Throughout January, fleet changes came fast and furious. Stagecoach received the first 5 of their new Alexander-bodied Mercedes 709D minibuses, placing them in service at Inverness where 7 Freight Rover Sherpas, 2 Leyland Leopards and 5 of the tri-axle Talbot Pullmans on loan from Cumberland were withdrawn. Also taken out of service at Perth and Dundee at the end of January were 11 Leyland Nationals, all of which were then moved to Spittalfield for storage. Many of these remained licensed however and were thus available for immediate reinstatement whenever this was found to be necessary. Another unexpected move saw the arrival from Ribble on 14 January of 8 former Greater Manchester Leyland Atlanteans which, in full corporate livery, were immediately allocated to Glasgow's Magicbus fleet. In exchange, 4 of Stagecoach's Bristol VRTs were on this same date despatched to Ribble where they were joined by 5 ECW-bodied Atlanteans from Cumberland. Ribble also acquired 2 Bristol VRTs from United Counties and transferred 13 of its delicensed vehicles to Cumberland's Barrow depot for storage. Cumberland sold its driver training FS6G-type Lodekka during January while conversely, Stagecoach relegated one of its Perth-based FLF6G Lodekkas to driver tuition duties and repainted it into an all-yellow livery.

On 19 January, Southdown hired a Wadham Stringer-bodied Leyland Swift from East Sussex County Council for use on an access-type service for which this vehicle was equipped with a wheelchair lift. More unexpectedly, East

One of a trio of NCME-bodied Leyland PD3/4 buses used by Southdown as driver training vehicles, FCD292D, smartly repainted into corporate livery also serves as a publicity vehicle when necessary. (T.G.Walker)

February had barely begun when, on the second day of the month, East Midland took a 50% holding in Maun International Coachways of Sutton in Ashfield, thus reducing the limited competition they had faced on a number of routes including that running from Mansfield to Newark. Maun International Travel Consultants Ltd. and Maun Crusader Tours Ltd. were excluded from the deal which added 19 single deckers and minibuses; 4 double deckers and 6 withdrawn vehicles to the East Midland fleet and gave them a new operating base at Sutton. Many of the vehicles transferred were, mainly due to their age and condition, condemned immediately, and to compensate, 1 Bristol VRT, 3 Leyland Nationals and an Alexander bus-bodied Leyland Tiger were transferred from East Midland to the Maun fleet as well as occasional loans of other types including a Routemaster. In addition, 2 DAFs, an AEC Reliance and a Dodge S56 minibus were operated for a short period from Maun International Travel Consultants Ltd. until some service adjustments could be made to reduce the vehicle requirement. In view of East Midland only owning a 50% stake in the Sutton-based business, Maun was operated independently and retained its colourful green, cream, orange & red livery.

Further north, Cumberland closed its Ulverston depot on 16 February, moving its 6-vehicle allocation to Cumbria Commercials' yard in the town while in Carlisle, a start was made on the demolition of part of the bus station behind which a new bus station was to be built on approximately the site of the old Western SMT depot and terminal. Reintroducing an almost forgotten practice, Cumberland began to fit all its Barrow-based buses with coloured destination blinds, using a range of different colours for the various routes.

The first Hastings & District vehicle to be repainted into the new corporate livery was East Lancs-bodied Leyland Atlantean 518 which after being painted all-over white early in the month received its stripes on 25 February. A few days prior to this, for reasons unknown, several Hastings & District Buses had green Southdown names (of bus stop sign size) and logo added to their front panel, although these were all removed before the month ended. At around this same time, Timtronic ticket machines were fitted to all the

former Portsmouth Citybus conventional-size vehicles in place of their former Magnet machines which were then only used on the minibuses. Meanwhile, on 25 February, Southdown launched two new minibus services between Chichester and Witterings - numbered 252/253 - in order to retaliate against Westrings of West Wittering who had for some time offered competition on this corridor, and for these adopted the new brand name 'Coastline'. Soon afterwards, Southdown won the tender for the park and ride scheme in Chichester placing this too under the Coastline banner and this name was gradually extended to all the company's minibuses operating from Chichester (including Bognor) in the same way that the Cedarbus name was used in Worthing.

In Scotland, Magicbus moved from its old depot at Warroch Street, Glasgow on 25 February to new premises at Hobden Street in the Springburn area of the city. Comprising a modern maintenance workshop, office accommodation and a large open air parking area, this site provided the company with much improved facilities and more space even though it was further away from the city centre. In Perth, a breakthrough in the bus war was finally achieved following talks between Stagecoach and Strathtay Scottish. Both companies agreed to share operations on each route on a 50/50 basis and co-ordinate their timings on Perth city services. The first route to be subject to this 'work sharing and co-ordinated timetable' agreement was that operating through the city centre from Hillend to Scone. This was the first time there had been any 'let-up' since the 'war' began and it was agreed by both parties that further co-operation

Left : One of Southdown's Chichester-based Robin Hood-bodied Iveco minibuses, 920 (G420RYJ) carries 'Coastline' fleet names and was on 6 March 1990 being used on service 25 in its home town. (Ian Buck)

Below : Receiving attention in Magicbus's Warroch Street depot, Glasgow in November 1989 were Stagecoach Bristol FLF6G Lodekka 085 (HGM335E) and Perth Panther-liveried Leyland National 214 (GTL352N). (K.A.Jenkinson)

would become a reality in the months ahead. This was a major achievement as Stagecoach had thus gained 50% of the Perth bus market after a seven-month war, having had 0% at the start. Having achieved its initial objective, Stagecoach's attention then moved to implementing the joint working agreement with Strathtay and scaling down the level of over provision that had built up during the bus war. In the meantime, a further 20 new Alexander-bodied Mercedes 709D minibuses had been licensed for service and were allocated to Tayside and Inverness. Those at the latter. in addition to wearing Stagecoach corporate colours, had Inverness Traction's 'IT' logos added to their sides and front to maintain the local identity, and replaced 5 of the hired tri-axle Talbot Pullmans which were then returned to Cumberland. The arrival of the new Mercedes minis at Perth and Dundee allowed 12 of the Devon General Ford Transits to be returned to their rightful owner. Although almost all of the Devon General buses had been used on Perth city services during their stay north of the border, one had been

This elevated view of the yard at Magicbus's former Cotters depot at Warroch Street, Glasgow on 24 February 1990, the day before its closure, shows Bristol Lodekkas, Routemasters and ex.Ribble Atlanteans, types which typified Stagecoach's Strathclyde area fleet at that time. (K.A.Jenkinson)

Below : A Sunday scene in the spacious yard of Magicbus's Hobden Street, Glasgow depot in April 1991 shows a selection of Routemasters, Bristol VRTs and ex.Ribble Atlanteans all enjoying their day of rest. (S.A.Jenkinson)

Inverness Traction's Alexander-bodied Mercedes 709D G281TSL, seen here in its home town soon after its entry into service at first carried fleet number 6. Later, it was renumbered into the Stagecoach minibus series, becoming 281.

In addition to being used regularly on service, hired Devon General Ford Transit C676FFJ was latterly used as the 'tea bus' at Mill Street, Perth, a duty it was performing when caught by the camera on 27 October 1989.   (K.A.Jenkinson)

used for a few weeks in Dundee whilst another had served as a staff 'tea bus' at Mill Street, Perth. Also departing from Perth were 3 Robin Hood-bodied Iveco 49.10s which were transferred to Southdown and a trio of Volvo coaches which were despatched to Inverness Traction who in turn withdrew one of its Leyland Leopards. Another stranger to arrive at Perth was an all-white liveried East Lancs-bodied Dodge S56 minibus which was transferred from Ribble.

Having never proved to be capable of operating the very hilly Castlemilk route for which they were obtained by Magicbus, 3 of the ex.Greater Manchester/Ribble Atlanteans were delicensed and sent to Spittalfield to join the reserve fleet which also gained another trio of Leyland Nationals now surplus to requirements. Another of the ex.Ribble Atlanteans - 116 - sustained accident damage while operating Magicbus service 20 in mid-February and as a result was despatched to Spittalfield for cannibalisation along with a further accident victim, ex.London Routemaster 604. On a happier note, the former Northern General front entrance Routemaster which had languished at Spittalfield since receiving accident damage in October 1989 was repaired and returned to service in Glasgow. Leaving Scotland were a Bristol FS6G which was sold to Skill, Nottingham for use as a driver training vehicle and two more Routemasters which departed to join East Midland's growing fleet of this type.

South of the border, Ribble withdrew 6 Leyland Nationals, 7 Leyland Leopards and 2 ex.Barrow Dodge S56 minibuses and sold its 1934 Leyland LT5A chassis to the Ribble Vehicle Preservation Society after taking a decision not to restore it themselves. Licenced for the first time was Mercedes minibus 530 (D672SHH) which, since its arrival in 1986 had been used as an experimental project by Ribble Engineering to produce a body suitable for fitting to this type of chassis. Being incomplete at the time of Ribble Engineering's closure, it was finished by Cumbria Commercials at their Carlisle workshops.

Towards the end of the month, work began on the transformation of Hastings & District Park Royal-bodied AEC Regent V from a driver training vehicle to full PSV status to enable it to be used in a passenger-carrying role on special

Superbly restored in the old Hastings & Distrtict livery of blue, cream & yellow for use on special PSV duties is former driver MFN946F, a Park Royal-bodied AEC Regent V.   (P.T.Stokes)

The only Leyland National to be adorned with the Magicbus fleet name was 205 (NEL857M) which carried this above its entrance door. Its passenger-carrying days ended, it awaits its fate at Stagecoach's Spittalfield graveyard in October 1990. (K.A.Jenkinson)

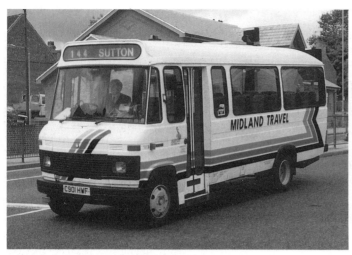

Painted in Stagecoach corporate colours, East Midland's ex.Maun Dormobile-bodied Mercedes 709D minicoach D322MNC carries the Midland Travel fleet name and is based at Shirebrook depot where it is seen here on 25 October 1990. (K.A.Jenkinson)

About to call at Mansfield bus station on an extremely wet day in September 1990 is Blackpool-bound Midland Travel Duple Laser-bodied Leyland Tiger 46 (NIB5455). Originally registered A46YAK, it was purchased new by East Midland in 1984. (P.T.Stokes)

East Midland 39, an Alexander-bodied Leyland Tiger coach in Stagecoach corporate livery with Mansfield & District fleet names rests in front of Shirebrook depot on 25 October 1990. Although on this occasion preparing to operate a works service, the banner heads in its side windows indicate its more normal use on the Sheffield to Nottingham express service. (K.A.Jenkinson)

occasions. Instead of receiving Stagecoach's corporate livery as might have been expected, it was painted into the attractive pre-takeover blue, cream & yellow Hastings colours to which old-style H & D fleet names were added. Earlier, and less happy, on 7 February one of the company's Mercedes minibuses - 806 - was severely damaged in an accident involving a skip lorry and as a result was withdrawn for cannibalisation.

On 5 March, East Midland and Rainworth Travel combined their coaching and travel agency activities and Rainworth's bus operations into a new division of East Midland which, operating as Rainworth Travel Ltd., used the trading name 'Midland Travel'. The 'new' company and its combined 35-vehicle was based at East Midland's Shirebrook depot, thus allowing the old Rainworth premises at Langwith to be closed and offered for sale. East Midland loaned another four MCW Metrorider minis to London Buses in exchange for those loaned in January while Rainworth had acquired 1 Volvo and 6 Leyland Tiger coaches from East Midland immediately prior to being relaunched under the Midland Travel banner. More surprising however was the appearance of East Midland's Plaxton Paramount 3500-bodied Leyland Tiger 56 (B56DKW) on a number of publicity duties in Midland Travel Coachstyle livery carrying the registration MTC345 despite this mark not being owned by the company. It never ran in service in this guise of course and later regained its correct identification before resuming its normal passenger-carrying duties.

March proved to be a month during which Stagecoach faced criticism in both Preston and Portsmouth following their acquisition of local operators. Concern was expressed by Lancashire County Council at the deterioration in the standard of service by Ribble in the Preston area where

difficulties had arisen following the acquisition of tendered contracts from Mercers of Longridge. The additional pressure on vehicles, and particularly the need for additional double deckers had severely strained Ribble's resources and as a result the company gave notice of termination of five of the County Council's contracts. In Portsmouth it was announced that an investigation was to be mounted by the Monopolies and Mergers Commission into the Group's acquisition of Portsmouth Citybus where the Secretary of State for Trade and Industry believed that this had possible effects on competition in the market for commercial and contracted bus services. The MMC was asked to make its report by May 21, and although there was confidence in the Southdown camp, the outcome of the report was awaited with some trepidation. Meanwhile, Stagecoach were not surprised to learn that the Office of Fair Trading was not going to take up the complaint lodged by Strathtay Scottish relating to Magicbus' competitive activities in the Perth area since any innovative practices undertaken by the Stagecoach Group were always more than matched by equally innovative practices by Strathtay, and in any event the work sharing agreement had rendered the whole matter irrelevant.

Strengthening its management team in southern England, Stagecoach appointed John Chadwick, former managing director of Solent Blue Line, to the position of area manager for Hampshire Bus's Basingstoke operation. This post had remained vacant since the departure of its previous holder, Piers Marlow to People's Provincial at the end of 1989.

Further increasing its fleet of double deckers, UTI, which in March was renamed Stagecoach Malawi, acquired via the Group's Hong Kong associate, Speedybus Enterprises, 6 more Metsec-bodied Daimler CVG6s from Kowloon Motor Bus Co. The arrival of these - via the customary route - allowed double deckers to be introduced to Lilongwe's Cityline services in March 1990. The first new buses for the Malawi subsidiary were also ordered at this time, these being 28 Gardner-engined ERF Trailblazers. To be supplied in ckd form for local assembly, it was hoped that these new chassis could be bodied locally by PEW of Malawi, a coachbuilding company in which Stagecoach Malawi had a 14% stake, but if this could not be undertaken quickly, the bodies would be

Being hoisted aboard a container in Hong Kong harbour at the start of its long journey to Malawi on 22 March 1990 is former Kowloon Motor Bus Co. Metsec-bodied Daimler CVG6 D543. One of its sisters is already safely stowed ready to be floated out for transfer to the ship which will carry them to Durban. (C.Lau)

Stagecoach Malawi 447, one of six ERF Trailblazers fitted with towing hooks for use in the 'Express' fleet is seen at Blantyre, with its freight trailer attached, being used for driver familiarisation purposes soon after its entry into service in 1990. (Stagecoach Malawi)

built by AUT of Harare. Operationally, Stagecoach Malawi continued to review its service network and improved the frequency on most of its Express services and re-introduced its route from Blantyre to Monkey Bay to cater for Lake travellers and tourists. The intercity service to Kasungu and Mzimba was extended to Mchinji, Mzuzu and Karonga whilst the Night Express to Karonga proved to be increasingly popular despite being limited to dry season operation. The long-awaited extension of Coachline from Lilongwe to Mzuzu (3 days a week) and from Zomba to Blantyre (daily) started on 26/27 November to herald further improvements planned for the new decade.

A massive fleet reorganisation took place north of the border during March following the arrival of another 29 new Alexander-bodied Mercedes minibuses. Of these, 21 were allocated to Inverness Traction where they were used to replace a number of Freight Rover Sherpas and 2 Volvo coaches and joining them in north west Scotland was the ex.Highwayman Mercedes mini, A121XWB. The remaining 8 of the new Mercedes were sent to join the Magicbus fleet at Glasgow for use mainly on the Castlemilk service. Given full Magicbus fleet names, these were the first minibuses to be regularly used by the company in the Strathclyde area and to compensate for their arrival, the remaining four ex. Ribble Atlanteans were removed from service and placed in store together with an Alexander-bodied Leopard.

As a result of the reduced frequency introduced to the Scone service in Perth and the arrival during the previous month of a number of new Mercedes minibuses, several of the original Perth Panther Robin Hood-bodied Ivecos were removed from service and despatched to other Stagecoach subsidiaries with 5 passing to United Counties and 2 to Southdown. The remaining 8 of the Devon General Ford Transits were also taken out of use and were returned to their owner on 21 March. To take up the short fall created by this large number of departures, two more East Lancs-bodied ex.Barrow Dodge S56 minibuses were acquired from Ribble together with a Robin Hood-bodied Iveco 49.10 from Hampshire Bus. Meanwhile, Bristol Lodekkas once again

Wearing Magicbus fleet names, Alexander-bodied Mercedes 709D minubus 300 (G300TSL) rests at Hobden Street depot, Glasgow after ending its duty on the 68 service on 18 March 1990. (K.A.Jenkinson)

Basking in the August 1990 sunshine at Spittalfield depot, these two former Cumberland Plaxton-bodied Leopards have both hidden their identity beneath Stagecoach cherished numbers. 4585SC began life as ACH141H and is currently registered RSH832H while 2412SC was originally ACH142H and is now 147YFM, having been RSH831H for two months at the end of 1990. (K.A.Jenkinson)

featured in the news when a pair of FLF6Gs were taken out of store at Spittalfield and were returned to service at Perth and the unused FS6G purchased from preservationists some eleven months earlier was moved to Inveralmond depot where it replaced the former Cumberland Bristol VRT as a store. The VRT was then taken to Spittalfield for gradual cannibalisation. Another FLF6G - LLJ443F - was withdrawn and immediately sold to a dealer, but more surprisingly, the Lodekka equipped as a mobile caravan which had been purchased in this form by Stagecoach in December 1986 was prepared for a number of trips to Romania, driven by Spittalfield staff. Although most definitely not equipped to PSV specification, this bus was nevertheless repainted into full Stagecoach livery (albeit minus fleetnames) in order to promote the Group's worldwide interests.

A total of 17 of Inverness Traction's withdrawn Freight Rover Sherpa minibuses, some of which had been temporarily stored at Spittalfield, were offered for sale by auction in Manchester by their leasing company owners and

Above : Replacing the ex.Cumberland Bristol VRT as a store at Stagecoach's new Inveralmond, Perth depot was Bristol FS-type Lodekka 069 (TVL307). Behind it, Alexander-bodied Leopard XGM460L was used as a uniform store. (K.A.Jenkinson)

Left : Repainted into corporate livery, Bristol FLF6G mobile caravan FJB738C made several 'aid' trips to Romania during 1990. (K.A.Jenkinson)

Below : Yellow-liveried ex.Southdown Bedford 'Green Goddess' recovery wagon Q995AFG rests at Stagecoach's Perth depot in March 1990 before being despatched to Inverness to take up its new duties. (K.A.Jenkinson)

only two of these failed to find buyers. Another former Inverness vehicle which had reclined at Spittalfield for several weeks since its withdrawal - Leopard L14 - had a less rosy future however and was sold to Dunsmore (breaker) of Larkhall before the month ended.

Continuing the long-established policy of re-registering its vehicles with dateless numbers, convertible open top Lodekka 866NHT donated its number to Volvo coach 407 (LUA250V), gaining in its place XSL227A. Another bus to lose its original plates was Routemaster 610 (397CLT) which, upon its transfer to East Midland was re-registered OWJ871A. Completing the changes in Scotland was the arrival of a former 'Green Goddess' Bedford RL towing wagon from Southdown which, after being repainted in an all-yellow livery, was despatched to Inverness depot.

Elsewhere in the Stagecoach empire, Cumberland had at the end of February withdrawn its unique pair of ECW-bodied Bristol LHS6L buses which had originated from Ribble and on 12 March suffered the loss of Leyland National 377 when this was involved in an accident with Brownrigg of Egremont's Bedford PWR646K on the A595 near Thornhill. Another accident victim was Hampshire Bus 205, an Alexander-bodied Olympian which lost its roof beneath the low Worting Arch at Basingstoke while working a bingo contract during the latter part of March.

A TIME OF CONSOLIDATION

April witnessed the continued restructuring of the Group's subsidiary fleets and following the arrival of 5 new Alexander-bodied 85-seat Leyland Olympians in March, Southdown received a further 5 identical buses in April. Added to these were a pair of Robin Hood-bodied Iveco minibuses from Perth Panther, one of which arrived via Hampshire Bus. On the debit side, Southdown despatched four of its convertible open-top Bristol VRTs to Cumberland who placed them in service in the Lake District surprisingly still wearing their apple green and cream livery and transferred a further pair together with a conventional VRT to

During the early part of April, Maun International Coachways Ltd. had been renamed Maun Buses Ltd. in order to indicate its complete separation from Maun International Travel Consultants and at the same time, one of its Leyland Leopards and a dual purpose-seated Mercedes 609D mini were transferred to East Midland's Midland Travel fleet.

North of the border, Inverness Traction withdrew from service two more of its Freight Rover Sherpas, replacing them with a pair of new Alexander-bodied Mercedes MB709Ds. Magicbus received three more ECW-bodied

Southdown's apple green & cream livery was adopted by Cumberland for its 'Lakeland Experience' fleet which operated tourist services in South Lakeland. Seen at Ambleside on 26 May 1990 during its first season with Cumberland is 2038 (UWV620S), a former Southdown open-top Bristol VRT. (B.K.Pritchard)

One of East Midland's Reeve Burgess-bodied 25-seat Iveco 49.10s, 916 (G916KWF) which carries Maun Minibus fleet names, leaves Mansfield bus station on a local service on 3 June 1991. (K.A.Jenkinson)

Hampshire Bus as replacements for three VRTs destroyed by fire at Basingstoke depot on 26 April. One of the latter was later repaired and returned to service whilst the other two were so badly damaged that they were dismantled for scrap. Southdown's Duple 425 coach 1185 left the fleet to join Hastings & District, although it was not placed in service by its new owner until mid-June, and a pair of dual-purpose Leopards were loaned to Leicestershire independent, Kinch of Barrow upon Soar. Also leaving their south coast home was a large number of the Atlanteans acquired with the Portsmouth Citybus business, these travelling northwards to meet their fate in the yard of Ripley (breaker) at Carlton near Barnsley. Following the arrival of a pair of Robin Hood-bodied Ivecos from Perth Panther, Hampshire Bus withdrew its unique Wright-bodied Dodge minibus D365OSU placing it in store at Southdown's Hilsea depot, and transferred one of its own Iveco 49.10s to Perth. A further Perth Panther Iveco was transferred to United Counties while in the north midlands, Rainworth Travel re-registered six of its Leyland Tiger coaches and two Bedford YNVs with Northern Ireland numbers in the 'NIB' series and East Midland acquired an Alexander bus-bodied Leopard from Maun Buses.

The premises of Ripley (breaker), Carlton in 1990 revealed ex.Maun Fleetline AAL179A (originally 77RTO) and a number of former Portsmouth CityBus Atlanteans - including 289 - awaiting the scrapman's torch. (P.T.Stokes)

Bristol VRTs which, upon their arrival from East Midland replaced two Routemasters and a Leyland Leopard while two of the former Inverness Traction Alexander-bodied Leopards were transferred to Cumberland for eventual use as driver training vehicles. Despite having well-equipped workshops at Whitehaven, Cumberland surprisingly sent two accident-damaged Leyland Nationals (377 & 861) to Go Ahead Northern for repair, this work being carried out at Gateshead during the early part of April. Another vehicle to travel in a southerly direction across the border was Stagecoach's converible open-top Bristol FS6G Lodekka, 866NHT which, shortly before its departure had been re-registered XSL228A. Having mainly been used for driver training purposes at Perth during its latter months north of the border, this Lodekka, still in its all-white livery was given a new home by Hampshire Bus to whose Basingstoke depot it was delivered early in April.

Above : Unique within the Stagecoach Group's corporate fleet is D365OSU, a former Strathclyde PTE Wright-bodied Dodge GO8 minibus fitted with a rear tail lift. Seen at Basingstoke on 27 January 1990 whilst a member of the Hampshire Bus fleet, it looked neat in its corporate livery as it operated a journey to South View on service 317. (Ian Buck)

Left : A view of the yard at Hampshire Bus's Basingstoke depot in May 1990 shows from left to right : Bristol VRT 410 which had been decapitated in an accident, former Stagecoach convertible open-top Bristol FS6G XSL228A (formerly 866NHT), Leyland PD3/4 driver trainer HCD360E and Bristol VRT 370. (Travelscene)

As a result of a management restructuring exercise, several changes were made within Magicbus's Highland division at Inverness following the departure of its manager, Malcolm Vaughan who had founded the original Inverness Traction company. Replacing him were Iain Cartwright who was appointed as traffic manager after spending the previous 17 years with Highland Scottish and John Hodkinson who had moved from Ribble to become commercial manager. John Service who had previously been with Perth-based Tayside Travel Services (formerly Stagecoach Express Services) replaced Frank Steven as fleet engineer. In Africa, Peter Lutman took up the position of managing director of Stagecoach Malawi at the start of April after having spent three weeks earlier in the year acting in a consultancy capacity on the replanning of the company's operations in and around Blantyre. One of his first duties was to increase double deck bus operation in Lilongwe following the outstanding success of such vehicles in Blantyre, and in preparation for this a further 6 Daimler CVG6s were acquired

from Kowloon during April with 4 more following in May. The Southern, Central and Northern 'Country' networks continued to change as Inter-City expanded to take the place of tar-road routes and 'Country' buses now covered every corner of Malawi including (rains permitting) Nyika Plateau. Most visible to the urban population however was 'Cityline' (and the Blantyre/Limbe 'Forestline' networks) which had made urban travel much easier for the 1990s. In addition, 'Cityline' services were introduced in the Zomba municipality for the first time.

Back home, Hampshire Bus was facing problems in Basingstoke where the local council were to implement a controversial one way traffic scheme. This, it was said, would seriously affect Hampshire Bus's operations in the town and to emphasise this point, the company commissioned a survey which led to an alternative contra-flow bus lane proposal being submitted to the council. Despite this being supported by a Department of Environment inspector, this was turned down by the powers that be who insisted upon

Being dismantled in Stagecoach's Spittalfield graveyard in March 1990 are Routemasters 628DYE and 838DYE which were withdrawn from service in March 1989 and April 1988 respectively. (K.A.Jenkinson)

One of the former East Midland Bristol LH6Ls, SNU851R was transferred to Stagecoach, Perth in October 1989 before moving a few weeks later to join the fleet of Hampshire Bus with whom it is seen here at Basingstoke bus station on 24 February 1990. In January 1991, it was despatched north of the border for the second time, on this occasion to Inverness.   (Ian Buck)

About to leave Windermere on its journey from Ambleside to Bowness on 2 September 1990 is Cumberland ABV669A, an ex.Ribble former Devon General open-top Leyland Atlantean in its new owner's Lakeland Experience apple green & cream livery.   (B.K.Pritchard)

the implementation of their original scheme. As a result, Hampshire Bus ceased to serve the town's railway station on outward journeys and no longer operated southbound along New Road on services 18 and 323, causing considerable inconvenience to passengers.

Following its blockade of Keswick bus station in August 1988 after a dispute with the local council who blocked the development plans of Conder Developments to whom the site was sold by Cumberland Motor Services in November 1988, Condor resold this during the following year to Caterite, the council's preferred buyer, for the construction of a supermarket. Rumours then began to circulate that Cumberland Motor Services was set to sell its bus stations at Whitehaven and Workington for redevelopment, gaining the anger of one of the area's Members of Parliament. Although the company refused to comment, both were prime sites near the centre of the towns concerned and would obviously attract high prices from developers. Meanwhile, the depots at Grange over Sands and Ulverston, both of which had already been closed, were placed on the market and the three buses based at Grange continued to be parked overnight on local car parks.

On 7 April, East Midland purchased the remaining 50% share of Maun Buses Ltd. to give them complete control of this company which continued to be operated as a separate subsidiary.   A number of service revisions were also implemented by East Midland which resulted in appreciable savings being made throughout the company, and changes to routes operated by Chesterfield and Clowne depots coincided with the introduction of new tendered work for Derbyshire County Council, an area in which the company had achieved modest gains. Meanwhile, the investigation by the Office of Fair Trading into Ribble's acquisition of Mercers' stage carriage interests concluded that it was not necessary to refer this to the Monopolies and Mergers Commission, an outcome which was no doubt received by Stagecoach with some relief.

The co-ordination on Tayside between Magicbus and Strathtay Scottish took another step forward on 16 April when the competition in Perth was further scaled down with both companies co-ordinating their city services. This led to Magicbus reducing its Tayside fleet from 94 to 80 vehicles and Strathtay withdrawing some of its Routemasters and to Perth inner and outer circle services 5, 6, 9 & 10 being operated jointly by both companies on Mondays to Saturdays. Magicbus also revised their services 14 and 15, starting these at Scott Street, Perth instead of Kinnoull Street and slightly altering their timings. At this same time, Magicbus (Scotland) Ltd. applied to increase its vehicle licences from 140 to 160 and whilst this was granted, it was subject to the additional 20 vehicles being based at Perth and was accompanied by a warning from the Scottish Traffic Commissioner about maintenance at the company's Glasgow and Inverness depots. It was stated that since Magicbus' formation in 1986, 36 immediate prohibition notices - 14 of which indicated neglect - had been served on the company's buses, many of which were somewhat elderly or had been acquired from Inverness Traction. In their defence, Magicbus stated that all of the Inverness problems related to vehicles inherited from Inverness Traction, all of which had now been replaced and a massive investment programme had now been put in motion under which its entire minibus fleet had been replaced and that the recent move to new premises in Glasgow would lead to improved maintenance. The final day of the month saw Magicbus cut its Dundee area service 74 back from Arbroath to Carnoustie, thus abandoning the extension added on 22 January and Strathtay withdrew its duplication operated against remaining Stagecoach buses operating routes 74 and 75.

At the other end of the country, Hastings & District began operating as 'Hastings Buses' on 17 April and introduced a new service network under which all Top Line's routes passed to the Hastings company together with Top Line's 17 Leyland Nationals. Immediately before this reorganisation, Hastings & District withdrew from service 1 Leyland National, 1 Bristol RELH, 8 Bristol RELLs, 2 dual-purpose Leyland Leopards and 13 Mercedes L608D minibuses, passing 12 of the latter to Southdown for further service. The Eastbourne & District minibus operations of Hastings & District were transferred from Hastings depot to Southdown's Eastbourne base from this same date and as a result, Mercedes

Hastings & District Duple-bodied Leopard 1154 (472YMF originally CKR154T) in Hastings Coaches yellow, cream & blue livery rests at Southsea in January 1990 whilst undertaking a private hire duty. (Travelscene)

minibuses 846-52 all had their Eastbourne & District stickers removed.

Stagecoach Holdings' financial year ending 30 April 1990 produced a profit of £4.217 million and the company's accounts revealed the individual figures of each of the group's subsidiary companies. Ribble showed a profit before interest of £441,000 on a turnover of £19.454 million; East Midlands had a profit of £578,000 on a £15.625 million turnover and United Counties a profit of £1.259 million on a turnover of £14.874 million. Cumberland returned £1.666 million on a £14.481 million turnover; Southdown and its subsidiaries nil profit on a turnover of £12.401 million; and Hampshire Bus made a profit of £732,000 on its £6.47 million turnover whilst Magicbus showed a loss of £544,000 on its turnover of £3.335 million, reflecting undoubtedly restructuring costs associated with the sale of the express operations to Caledonian Express and the takeover of the loss-making Inverness Traction business. Stagecoach's overseas operations brought £1,314 million profit from a turnover of £11.741 million. Also shown were the prices paid for Stagecoach's major acquisitions during the financial year, these being £6.326 million for Southdown, £663,000 for Portsmouth Citybus and £1.165 million for Hastings & District. Ann Gloag and Brian Souter each held 9.988 million 10p shares in Stagecoach Holdings Ltd. and no other directors had any interest in shares in the company at 30 April 1990.

The highlight of the year was however the announcement that Ann Gloag, Stagecoach Holdings managing director, had been awarded the Institute of Directors sponsored 'Business Woman of the Year Award' after being an unsuccessful short listed candidate the previous year. More usually awarded to someone working in the fashion, cosmetic or retail trades, it was fitting that transport - which was not nearly as glamourous - had at last been recognised and even more fitting that the recipient should be someone

who had in such a short space of time done so much to change the face of the bus and coach industry.

The month of May, not surprisingly, brought with it the customary reshuffling of vehicles amongst the various subsidiary fleets as well as witnessing the arrival of more new Alexander-bodied Mercedes minibuses. Allocated to Inverness (4), Glasgow (2) and Perth (5), the arrival of the latter allowed the withdrawal of a similar number of Perth Panther Iveco 49.10s which then travelled south to join Hampshire Bus. One of these stayed but a few days with its new owner however before being transferred to Southdown. Moving in the opposite direction were two more Hampshire Bus Iveco minibuses which were added to the Perth-based fleet and an AEC Matador recovery wagon which was placed in store at Spittalfield to await its eventual call to duty. A further ancillary vehicle to travel northwards was a fuel tanker transferred from Ribble to Inverness where it was used to maintain a supply of the necessary liquid to the locally-based fleet pending construction of a permanent fuel bunkering facility. Its duties completed, this tanker was then despatched to East Midland. Another five Bristol VRTs arrived in Scotland from East Midland and were joined by two more buses of this type from United Counties, one of

On hire to Moffat & Williamson for use on a special service to Perth Racecourse on 21 August 1989, Stagecoach Bristol FLF6G 081 (GDL769E) rests between duties at Moffat & Williamson's Gauldry depot alongside one of that operator's ECW-bodied Daimler Fleetlines which was, coincidentally, acquired from Ribble, another member of the Stagecoach group, in 1988. (S.K.Jenkinson)

Still wearing its Scottish Stagecoach fleet name as it travels through Andover in June 1990 on service 294 to Foxcotte is Hampshire Bus 36 (G36SSR), a Phoenix-bodied Iveco 49.10 which started life in the Perth Panther fleet. (A.Gilmour)

Resting in Bedford bus station and Iilustrating United Counties original dark green 'Street Shuttle' livery is 39 (D39DNH), a Robin Hood-bodied Iveco 49.10. (T.G.Walker)

which was immediately taken to Spittalfield for cannibalisation. Withdrawn by Magicbus were a Leyland Leopard and a Leyland National, the latter being immediately sold to an independent operator at Wishaw whilst more surprisingly, five Leyland Nationals were removed from store at Spittalfield and returned to service mainly on schools and works contract duties. The company's Routemaster fleet was further depleted by the transfer of 613 to East Midland for spares and one of Stagecoach's Alexander-bodied Leopards was despatched to Ribble for eventual use as a driver training bus. Ribble also gained from Magicbus a pair of Alexander-bodied Mercedes minis and three of the Atlanteans which had travelled north in January. Withdrawn by Ribble were 2 Robin Hood-bodied Ivecos, 2 Carlyle-bodied Freight Rover Sherpas, a Leyland National adapted to carry wheelchairs and an open top Atlantean. The latter two were transferred to Cumberland who were to repaint the Atlantean into Southdown apple green & cream livery to match the open top Bristol VRTs used in the Lake District. To assist Ribble following the closure of its central engineering workshops some months earlier, Cumberland began to undertake M.O.T work on its vehicles at its Kendal depot and a steady flow of buses from various Ribble depots were soon to be seen travelling to and from the town for this purpose. Cumberland's Olympian Megadekka 1201 was loaned to United Counties towards the end of the month for use on a week's promotional duties while Southdown acquired an open-top PDR1/1-type Atlantean from Southampton CityBus and hired a wheelcair lift-equipped Wadham Stringer-bodied Leyland Swift from East Sussex County Council. Finally, Hampshire Bus Bristol VRT 410 was de-roofed when on 21 May it became the latest victim of the low Worting Arch at Basingstoke.

Although a busy month as far as fleet movements were

Looking smart in its red & yellow livery with grey skirt, Ribble training bus TS2, a Marshall-bodied Leyland Leopard originally registered TRN477 and later TRN995A is seen at Morecambe depot on 22 August 1990 after having been re-registered yet again to become ABV785A. (K.A.Jenkinson)

concerned, May proved to be comparatively quiet in operational terms with few changes taking place. United Counties introduced more Street Shuttle minibuses to Corby with an increased frequency on route 2 to Kingsthorpe and route 5 to Stephenson Way and the introduction of a new service (numbered 7) which operated hourly, linking the town's bus station with Great Oakley and additionally began a new Street Shuttle service from Kettering to Rothwell on an hourly basis, numbering this 19B. Carlisle's new bus station was opened towards the end of the month and was considerably smaller than the previous terminal while East Midland sold its former Rainworth Travel depot at Langwith, to a firm manufacturing lamp posts.

FURTHER DEVELOPMENT OVERSEAS

During June, property was again in the news when United Counties moved its head office and depot in Northampton from Bedford Road to new premsies at Rothersthorpe Avenue and sold its original site for redevelopment into sheltered housing. Coming as a much greater surprise however was the announcement that Stagecoach Holdings had increased its overseas activities by the purchase of Gray Coach Lines of Canada from its municipal owner, Toronto Transit Commission for $16.1million (around £8 million), thus giving the Group its first foothold in North America. An old established company formed in 1927, Gray Coach Lines had a fleet of 98 coaches of MCI manufacture which dated from 1974 to 1988 and offices at 180 Dundas Street West, Toronto. Operating on three main groups of frequent inter-city scheduled express routes to Sudbury and North Bay in the north, Kitchener, Guelph and Owen Sound to the north-west of Toronto and to St.Catherines, Niagara Falls and Buffalo in the USA, Gray Coach also maintained the high frequency coach services to downtown Toronto from Pearson International Airport as well as the Toronto and Niagara Falls sightseeing tours. Under the guidance of its President, Bill Verrier who was to remain with Gray Coach, the company whilst not proposing to immediately alter its activities, began examining its operations with a view to future expansion in order to increase its present $30million turnover. Amongst these is the possibility of introducing open-top double deckers to the city and Niagara Falls sightseeing tours and to this end, a feasibility study was undertaken in Britain early in 1991 by East Midland at Chesterfield with the conversion of

an ex.Stagecoach Bristol Lodekka for this purpose. Meanwhile legal complexities in Canada prevented the company using the Stagecoach name, although advise is being solicited in an attempt to enable its use in the future, and to date the only concession to the company's new ownership has been the addition of Stagecoach's blue, red and orange stripes to the badges worn by Gray Coach's drivers. The purchase of Gray Coach Lines by Stagecoach was monumental in as much as it was one of the first major privatisation moves for the Canadian Transit industry.

Back in Scotland, the picture was not quite so rosy with Magicbus having lost its contract held for the provision of a two-bus working on the Glasgow - Lennoxtown route during the latest round of tendering in Strathclyde. Fortunately, this was countered by the success on Tayside where nine bus workings on school services were gained in Perth from Strathtay Scottish under new Tayside Regional Council tenders. On an even brighter note, Brian Souter was rewarded for his contribution to the passenger transport industry by being presented with the Scottish Young Business Achievement Award, a well-earned accolade which he richly deserved.

During June, Inverness Traction withdrew the last two of its inherited Freight Rover Sherpa minibuses and in addition lost two Alexander-bodied Mercedes which were sold to Ribble. Magicbus delicensed one of its FLF6G Lodekkas and sold an accident damaged Routemaster to Dunsmore (breaker) of Larkhall, a heavily cannibalised example to

Typifying the Gray Coach Lines fleet in Canada is 2523, a 1986 MCI 102A3-type three-axle coach. With seating for 47 passengers plus standee accommodation for a further 16, this type of coach is used on all the company's diverse operations and, as can be seen, carries three different registration plates above its front bumper.   (Stagecoach)

With the magnificent Niagara Falls forming the backdrop, Gray Coach Lines 1987-vintage MCI 102A3 three-axle coach 2535 undertakes a sightseeing tour to this major attraction in the spring of 1991. (Stagecoach)

Being cannibalised for spares at Stagecoach's Spittalfield graveyard in October 1990 are ex.United Counties Bristol VRT ANV776J which had never operated north of the border, ex.Cumberland Bristol VRT HHH273N and accident damaged ex.Ribble NCME-bodied Leyland Atlantean LJA600P. (K.A.Jenkinson)

Carrying the two-tone blue & yellow livery of Hastings & District, Alexander-bodied Mercedes L608D 828 carries the legend 'Rye Town Bus' across the top of its windscreen as it works a duty on the 348 service to Hastings town centre. (T.W.W.Knowles)

Wigley (breaker) of Carlton and transferred another bus of this type to Cumberland for use as a source of spares. Also leaving Scotland were a further Alexander-bodied Leopard and another Atlantean, both of which passed to Ribble where the former was destined to become a driver trainer and the latter was placed in service. Two of Perth Panther's Robin Hood-bodied Iveco 49.10s - including one of the pair acquired from Hampshire Bus during the previous month - were despatched to join Southdown who, in their place, sent a convertible open-top Bristol VRT to Perth where it was immediately put into service (with its roof fitted) still wearing its former owner's apple green & cream livery to which Stagecoach vinyls were added.

The now customary reshuffling of the group's minibuses continued with the loan on 23 June to Hampshire Bus by Ribble of 3 Dormobile-bodied Dodge S46s which in mid July moved to Southdown to whom they were officially transferred and the permanent reallocation of 2 of Ribble's Robin Hood-bodied Iveco 49.10s to Southdown. Ribble received 11 new Alexander-bodied Mercedes 709Ds which in addition to replacing the above, also allowed the withdrawal of 11 Freight Rover Sherpas and in addition a pair of Leyland

New to Ribble and later passing to Cumberland, ECW-bodied Bristol LHS6L FBV271W and its sister were both transferred to Stagecoach at Perth in July 1990. Pictured at Perth depot on 6 April 1991, it had earlier in the day been operating service 15 from Perth to Comrie, a route upon which these two buses are frequently to be found. (S.K.Jenkinson)

Nationals and 2 Atlanteans were also taken out of service. Moving northwards were a trio of Dodge S56 minibuses which were transferred from Hampshire Bus to Cumberland and in the opposite direction, an Alexander coach-bodied Leyland Tiger was despatched from Cumberland to Southdown. Cumberland also disposed of the last of its three ex.Southdown full-fronted Leyland PD3s which, having never been used since its acquisition, was heavily cannibalised before being sold to a Workington scrap dealer.

Almost unbelievably, Hampshire Bus Duple-bodied Dennis Javelin 802 which had twice previously been returned to Duple following accident damage was again despatched to Hendon for repair following a collision with a Volvo car near Stockbridge on 20 June. Indeed, it was almost as if this particular bus was to spend more time at its coachbuilders than in service with its owner !

The inter-fleet movement of vehicles continued unabated throughout August with comings and goings in almost every direction. Starting in Scotland, a second ex.Hampshire Bus Robin Hood-bodied Iveco 49.10 returned south when it was transferred to Southdown whilst a trio of almost-new Alexander-bodied Mercedes 709Ds were transferred to Ribble along with another Leyland Leopard which was to eventually be added to that company's driver training fleet. Magicbus's Olympian Megadekka left its native Glasgow to join the fleet of East Midland who in exchange provided the Scottish-based fleet with two more Bristol VRTs. Four of the Leyland Nationals recently reinstated at Spittalfield were again taken out of service and relegated to the strategic reserve fleet, their place surprisingly being taken by Cumberland's 2 ex.Ribble ECW-bodied Bristol LHS6L buses. The transfer of this pair was somewhat unexpected in view of the unpopularity of the previous vehicles of this type operated from Spittalfield.

In addition to receiving the three Mercedes minis from Magicbus, Ribble also placed 3 more new buses of this type in service and gained a trio of Reeve Burgess-bodied

Mercedes L608Ds from Cumberland which together allowed the withdrawal of 11 Dormobile-bodied Renault Dodges, five of which were then transferred to Southdown. Cumberland acquired an Alexander-bodied Leopard from Magicbus for driver training purposes and transferred one of its Olympian Megadekkas to its Barrow depot where it replaced 2 Atlanteans !

for this in the hands of Barrow depot whilst Kendal continued to undertake much of Ribble's M.O.T. work. Barrow, which had become the main storage point for both Ribble and Cumberland's delicensed vehicles, housed numerous buses and coaches held in reserve by both companies in addition to accommodating several examples awaiting disposal and its content changed frequently. After losing their Eastbourne &

Still sporting Stagecoach fleet names some six months after being transferred from Perth to Ribble Motor Services, ex.Devon General Bristol VRT 2045 (FDV784V) passes Blackburn railway station whilst operating a local works service during the summer of 1990. (J.K.Grime)

More new vehicles to arrive were 6 Plaxton Expressliner-bodied Volvo B10M coaches which, in National Express Rapide livery, were placed in service by United Counties and 8 Alexander-bodied Mercedes 709D minis - three of which were fitted with coach-type seats - for Hampshire Bus. Another stranger to appear was a Wadham Stringer Portsdown-bodied 33-seat Dennis Dart which was evaluated by Southdown from 27 July until 4 August. Hastings & District withdrew another of its Bristol RELLs from service together with 4 of its Mercedes L608D minibuses, but more surprisingly repainted one of its three remaining Bristol REs into the old blue, cream & yellow livery rather than in the corporate Stagecoach colours at that time being applied to the other members of the fleet. Finally, another 5 Daimler CVG6 double deckers arrived in Malawi from Kowloon Motor Bus Co.,Hokg Kong together with another Duple coach-bodied Albion EVK55CL from this same source.

Operationally, Cumberland withdrew its maintenance facilities from its Millom depot, placing future responsibility

District names upon their transfer from Hasings & District to Southdown in April, four of the latter's ex. Hastings Mercedes L608Ds regained Eastbourne & District titles which were fitted to their windows by mid-July to re-introduce a local identity to the area in which they operated. Across in Basingstoke, Hampshire Bus introduced open-top double deck tours around the town using one of its two ex.Southdown convertible open-top Bristol VRTs. Running during July and August, mainly to Wellington Country Park, this new venture proved to be extremely popular and attracted a healthy number of passengers.

July however, proved to be not a particularly happy month for the Stagecoach Group who fell foul of the Secretary of State for Trade and Industry, Nicholas Ridley. Despite an investigation by the Monopolies and Mergers Commission on Stagecoach subsidiary Southdown's acquisition of Portsmouth Citybus concluding that although this was against the public interest, there had been no adverse effect so far, and recommending that no temporary increase in

Southdown Portsmouth's all-white liveried ex.Ribble Dormobile-bodied Dodge S46 minibus 977 stands in Portsmouth on 19 January 1990, the day before the company's operations in the city were sold to Transit Holdings. (MG Photographic)

Leaving Southport in the evening twilight of 14 June 1989, Cumberland's Plaxton Paramount-bodied DAF 509 wears the yellow & tan Yeowarts livery which was later to become Cumberland's standard Coachline colour scheme. (Travelscene)

Stagecoach's new generation of minibuses - Alexander-bodied Mercedes 709Ds - replaced the Iveco 49.10s and most of the Leyland Nationals on Perth Panther services during 1990. Here, coach-seated 311 (G200PAO) arrives in Kinnoull Street, Perth on the 14 service from Pitcairngreen in October 1990. (K.A.Jenkinson)

Southdown's preserved 1922 Leyland G7 open-top double decker was transported to Perth for use at the wedding of Stagecoach's managing director, Ann Gloag. Beautifully restored to its original condition, it wears Southdown's traditional green & cream livery. (Travelscene)

service frequencies or reduction in fares should be made as predatory retaliation against competitors, Nicholas Ridley almost unbelievably over-ruled the MMC's findings and instructed Stagecoach Holdings to sell off part of its Portsmouth operations. The Director of Fair Trading was given two months to negotiate with Stagecoach and if an agreement could not be reached within this period of time, the Secretary of State would then use his powers to 'enforce appropriate remedies'. Not surprisingly, this decision infuriated Brian Souter, especially as Hampshire County and Portsmouth City Councils along with bus user groups and trade unions had been in favour of the merger between Southdown and Portsmouth Citybus and the fact that the MMC had found no evidence of anti-competitive behaviour. Indeed, if the merger had not taken place, Portsmouth Citybus would have undoubtedly ceased trading and left the residents of the town with a much lower standard of overall service.

Almost before the implications of the forced divestment of their Portsmouth interests had sunk in, Stagecoach learned that the Office of Fair Trading was to conduct an investigation into East Midland's acquisition of Maun Buses.

After being stored unused at Cumberland's Carlisle depot since its acquisition with the business of Palmer, Carlisle, Duple-bodied Ford R1114 RBA618R made its final journey to the yard of Ripley (breaker), Carlton where it is seen in January 1991. (P.T.Stokes)

In the meantime, although the Monopolies & Mergers Commission had found that Highland Scottish had acted in an uncompetitive manner against Inverness Traction, no remedial action was to be taken against them, ironically as a result of Stagecoach's acquisition of the Inverness independent placing that company in a stronger competitive position !

Following the traumatic events of July which, to an extent, were to reshape Stagecoach's future in certain areas, the month witnessed a much happier merger when, on the 27th the Group's managing director, Ann Gloag, married David McCleary at Perth's Church of the Nazarene. For this occasion, Southdown Portsmouth provided its preserved 1922 Leyland G7 open-top double decker as wedding transport and, suitably decorated, it, like the bride, looked superb. The G7 had been transported to Perth on a low-loader lorry rather than undertaking this extremely long journey under its own power.

Indeed, Scotland proved to be the area of most activity during August as far as the Stagecoach conglomerate was concerned with the rest of the country enjoying a comparatively quiet month in operational terms. On 5 August Magicbus slightly revised its local Sunday service operations in Perth to provide a half-hourly frequency on routes 1, 2 & 7 and an hourly service the 5, 6, 9 & 10, all of these starting at around 10.00am and finishing at 7.00pm and being mainly operated by minibuses. A week later, on 13 August, the company took over Strathtay Scottish's route 17 (Perth - Kintillo / Dunning) as a result of re-tendering but at the end of the month, under the co-ordination agreement with Strathtay, ceased operations on its Dundee - Blairgowrie service, a two-bus working, leaving that route solely to the SBG subsidiary. In return, Strathtay Scottish undertook to withdraw two buses, leaving Magicbus (Scotland) Ltd. as the sole operaor between Perth and Pitcairngreen and between Perth and Bridge of Earn. Following the acquisition of Alexander Greyhound of Dundee by Tayside Public Transport Co. Ltd. , its fleet was moved from its premises in East Dock Street to Tayside's spacious adjacent premises, leaving Stagecoach as the sole occupants of the old

One of the buses acquired with the operations of Barrow Borough Transport, Ribble 1449 (LEO734Y), an NCME-bodied Leyland Atlantean in corporate livery picks up its passengers on the now withdrawn service 150 in September 1989. (T.G.Walker)

implemented was the withdrawal of two of its old-established trunk routes, the 150 from Preston to Burnley and the 761 from Liverpool to Blackpool. Both were in future to be covered by various shorter--distance services and as a result, the end of yet another era was reached.

On the vehicle front, 15 new Alexander-bodied Olympians were received, 7 of which were placed in service by Ribble with the remaining 8 being added to the Cumberland fleet. The Ribble examples were 87-seaters while those for Cumberland had seating for 85 passengers and incorporated a luggage pen in their lower saloon. Cumberland also acquired 5 three year-old Plaxton Paramount 3500-bodied Volvo B10M coaches from Wallace Arnold of Leeds and instead of placing these in service, put them in store at Carlisle depot where they were to remain for several months. At this same time, Cumberland decided to adopt the Yeowart livery of yellow & tan for the whole of its coaching fleet and

Greyhound depot. With these having also been acquired by Tayside Public Transport, it was wondered whether Stagecoach would be able to continue to park their vehicles at this site, but following negotiations with the new owners, agreement was reached for their vehicles to remain there overnight and between duties.

South of the border, Ribble revised a number of its services on 28 August and amongst the changes

The last rear entrance Bristol Lodekka to operate in service with Stagecoach, FS6G BXA464B stands alongside FLF6G HGM335E, now preserved by its owners, at Spittalfield depot in August 1990. (S.A.Jenkinson)

repainted a number of Leyland Leopards and Volvos into these colours with the addition of the Coachline fleet name. 7 of the company's older Bristol VRTs were withdrawn and despatched to Barrow for store until their sale was completed, and as replacements, 2 Leyland Atlanteans were transferred from Ribble. Also leaving Ribble were more of its Dormobile-bodied Dodge S46 minibuses, several of which were transferred to Southdown whilst 1 was despatched to join Hampshire Bus who also took delivery of 2 new Alexander-bodied Mercedes 709Ds. Hastings & District withdrew 5 more of its Mercedes L608D minis and transferred one of these to Southdown and in return gained 4 Leyland Nationals - 2 from Southdown and 2 from Hampshire Bus.

41 (E935NBK), one of Hampshire Bus's Alexander-bodied Renault S56 minibuses with 'Hampshire MiniBus' fleet names applied to its corporate livery, stands in the yard of Andover depot on 27 July 1988. (Ian Buck)

Approaching The Hard bus station, Portsmouth in July 1990, Southdown Portsmouth's ex.Citybus former London Leyland National 204 (THX219S) was still painted in its previous owner's ivory & red livery complete with Citybus fleet names. (T.G.Walker)

In Scotland, the Bristol VRT fleet was further increased by the arrival in August of 4 buses of this type from East Midland which replaced two more ageing Lodekkas and a trio of Leyland Nationals. The latter were returned to store at Spittalfield while one of the Lodekkas - 085 (HGM335E) - which had been in the Stagecoach fleet since August 1981, was added to the company's small contingent of preserved vehicles and was renumbered 003. Hopefully, this vehicle will now have a secure future as a representative of a type of bus which did so much to enhance Stagecoach's fortunes during the company's formative years. A further surprise was the return to service of one of Magicbus' ex. London Routemasters - 602 - which had been stored at Spittalfield since its withdrawal in April. That this bus was reinstated to passenger-carrying duties was not nearly as surprising as the fact that, having received a complete overhaul and repaint, it was given Stagecoach fleet names rather than Magicbus titles and thus became the first Routemaster to carry this identity since the summer of 1987.

Although Stagecoach Holdings had added no more companies to its growing portfolio since its Canadian acquisition in June, the company was continually searching for further expansion and had submitted bids for all the Scottish Bus Group subsidiaries already placed on the market. In addition, upon hearing of the difficulties at that time facing National Welsh Omnibus Services Ltd. an investigation into this company was instigated with a view to its possible purchase. Unfortunately however, no agreement could be reached with the National Welsh management and Stagecoach withdrew its interest to leave Western Travel Ltd. to acquire part of the company with the remainder being retained by its present owners. While these abortive negotiations were taking place, Gray Coach Lines increased its fleet - albeit temporarily - when it leased two MCI coaches from Toronto Transit for a period of six months, thus increasing its fleet to 100 vehicles in order to meet its slightly-increased operating requirements.

In Sussex, Southdown caused a major storm among local residents when it announced plans to close its bus station and depot in Lewes town centre for redevelopment as a shopping complex. It proposed to relocate its maintenance and overnight parking facilities to a new site outside the town and replace the bus station with bus stops in many of the town's busy streets and stated that this was necessary in order to reduce costs. Residents and town councillors were however outraged by these plans, feeling that the impact of extra traffic on the already overcrowded streets would be very much against public safety and as a result, the planning application for change of use was referred to a Govenment inspector.

Meanwhile, Hampshire Bus had been busy reorganising its premises and on the first day of September closed its Andover depot in Anton Mill Road and moved to new premises at Livingstone Road on the Walworth Industrial Estate. A few days later, the company's outstation at Stockbridge was reopened and was located in the same yard in High Street as was used until October 1986. In East Sussex, following the successful operation of the summer Sunday and weekday evening timetable by Hastings & District, instead of reverting to normal winter schedules on 17 September as had been planned, the summer timetable was continued until 27 October.

In Lakeland where Stratford upon Avon-based tour specialists Guide Friday had made their debut at the start of the 1990 summer season, as a result of fierce competition by

One of United Counties' Plaxton Expressliner-bodied Volvo coaches, 89 (G389PNV) in National Express Rapide livery leaves Luton bus station in October 1990 enroute to Leeds & Bradford on National Express-contracted service 325. (T.G.Walker)

Cumberland - who it will be remembered gained 4 Southdown open-top Bristol VRTs and a former Ribble open-top Atlantean for use in this picturesque area - the company decided to withdraw its operations on 2 September rather than continue them through the winter as had originally been planned. Although Guide Friday had been extremely successful in almost all the other tourist areas in which they operated, they proved to be no match for the local Stagecoach group subsidiary who once again were to reign supreme around the southern lakes.

Following Ribble's service reorganisation towards the end of August, the company was able to implement a slight fleet reduction during the following month and took out of service 3 dual purpose-bodied Leopards, 8 Leyland Nationals and 19 Atlanteans. In addition, a large number of its minibuses which had been held in store for several months were disposed of with 22 Freight Rover Sherpas being sold to Carlyle Bus Centre at Birmingham and 8 Robin Hood-bodied Fiat 49.10s being transferred to United Counties. Hampshire Bus withdrew 3 of its Iveco 49.10s, 5 Reeve Burgess-bodied Dodge S56s plus a Bristol VRT and acquired a Leyland National from Southdown - who took 2 Iveco minibuses in exchange - and 3 Mercedes 608D minibuses from Hastings & District who itself received 3 Leyland Nationals from Southdown and a pair of ECW-bodied Bristol LH6Ls from Hampshire Bus. Cumberland withdrew 2 more of its Bristol VRTs and received 7 Alexander-bodied Mercedes 709Ds from Magicbus at Perth and Glasgow while East Midland evaluated an NCME--bodied Renault PR110.2 single decker

in service for four weeks. East Midland's coaching division, Midland Travel, increased its fleet with the acquisition from Wallace Arnold of 5 Plaxton-bodied Volvo B10M coaches and in addition started operating a pair of Neoplan Skyliner double deck coaches. The latter were only temporary additions to the fleet however, as both were likely to be despatched to Africa during 1991. In Scotland, Magicbus continued to use one of its ex. Ribble / Barrow East Lancs-bodied Dodge S56 minibuses (353 - D459BEO) as the staff 'tea bus' at Mill Street, Perth, a duty it had performed for several months.

During September, Magicbus fitted an internal on-bus moving message advertising system to six of its Alexander-bodied Mercedes minibuses used mainly on the Glasgow - Castlemilk service. This used an LED screen fitted at the front above the driver's partition and showed a flow of advertising messages which would generate additional revenue. At the end of this same month, East Midland held a spectacular open day at Mansfield depot with 84 assorted vehicles on display including representatives from the Stagecoach Group at Perth and Hastings. In total, several thousand people attended the event and almost £3,000 was raised for charity.

The exodus of Alexander-bodied Mercedes minibuses from Scotland continued in October when a further 2 were tranferred to Cumberland who also gained a Bristol FS6G

Lodekka driver training bus from United Counties for continued use in this role. As a result of the reorganisation of its services in the Bolton area on 15 October, Ribble reduced its fleet still further by withdrawing 11 more of its Iveco 49.10 minibuses along with a Mercedes L608D mini, 2 Leyland Nationals, 3 dual-purpose Leopards and 4 Atlanteans. The latter were the final examples of the large number of secondhand double deckers acquired by the company at the time of deregulation in 1986.

The only new vehicles to enter service within the group were 5 Alexander-bodied 85-seat Leyland Olympians which were allocated to United Counties and 5 which were added to the Hampshire Bus fleet. On the reverse side of the coin, Hastings & District withdrew another 5 of its Mercedes L608D minibuses and a Leyland Leopard, but acquired 2 Plaxton Paramount-bodied Leyland Tiger coaches from Southdown towards the end of the month. Southdown surprisingly removed the 'cherished' registration numbers from several of its Leyland Tiger coaches, reallocating some of these to Cedarbus's MCW Metroriders and transferring others to Cumberland for re-use. In anticipation of the sale of its Portsmouth operations, all the surplus vehicles stored in Southdown's Hilsea depot were moved to Horsham between 13 and 19 October and added to the growing number of withdrawn buses were two PMT-bodied Mercedes L608D minibuses. Hampshire Bus also took two more of its Dodge S56s out of service and transferred an Iveco to Southdown.

An unusual visitor to Perth was a 23-seat CVE Omni minibus which was borrowed from its manufacturer for evaluation on Panther city services. After only one day

Evaluated by Stagecoach in November 1990 was G208CHN, a CVE Omni minibus. After only one day in service at Perth however, it was relegated to 'staff shuttle' duties and is seen here at Inveralmond depot whilst used in this role. (Campbell Morrison)

however, as a result of a defective windscreen wiper, it was relegated to staff taxi duties between Mill Street and Inveralmond depot for the remainder of its two week stay in late October/early November. Following accident damage sustained in September, Plaxton Supreme II-bodied Volvo B58-61 coach 404 (BGG162S) was rebuilt using a Supreme IV front whilst former Inverness Traction Alexander-bodied

Stagecoach Plaxton Supreme II-bodied Volvo B58-61 404 (BGG162S) was fitted with a Supreme IV front after its involvement in an accident in September 1990. It is seen here in its rebuilt form in Mill Street, Perth on 26 April 1991 whilst working the afternoon school days only service 25 to Aberfeldy. (K.A.Jenkinson)

Leopard OGM602M was repainted into an all-over yellow livery for driver training purposes and was then immediately despatched on loan to Malcolm Vaughan's PSV Driving School at Inverness.

As a result of higher fuel prices caused by the escalating Gulf crisis, Hastings & District increased all its fares on 7 October and although this action was not immediately copied by other members of the Stagecoach Group, the situation was constantly monitored to allow similar moves to be made when it was felt necessary. Following the Department of Trade and Industry's instruction to Stagecoach regarding the disposal of its former Portsmouth Citybus company, several concerns expressed interest in acquiring this operation including Southern Vectis, People's Provincial and Transit Holdings. It was however to be several weeks before a buyer emerged, as will be revealed later in this story.

An unexpected move saw four of Magicbus' ex. London Routemasters taken out of store and given a complete overhaul and repaint at Spittalfield. Attired with Stagecoach fleet names, these buses, which were joined by 602 from

Glasgow, were then returned to service at Perth where they were put to work on city services alongside buses of the same type operated by Strathtay Scottish. This was the first time that the company had employed Routemasters on its city service network, their previous duties on Tayside being in the 1985-7 period when they were used on schools contracts and Stagecoach's rural routes.

Having disposed of a quantity of its own Routemasters during the previous year, it came as a surprise when the Stagecoach group purchased 8 former Western (Clydeside) Scottish buses of this type from a Carlton dealer at the beginning of November. These were immediately taken to East Midland for storage at its Mansfield and Chesterfield depots pending a decision regarding their future use and in the event only one has been retained for cannibalisation, the remainder returning from whence they were acquired. Cumberland bolstered its minibus fleet by obtaining two more Alexander-bodied Mercedes 709Ds from Magicbus and finally eliminated its white & red Coachline livery following the repainting of the last vehicles in these colours into the new yellow & tan combination derived from the former

The five Routemasters transferred from Magicbus to Stagecoach now operate Perth City Services alongside Bristol VRTs and Mercedes minibuses. Here, 614 (LDS210A) which was originally 245CLT and numbered 607, passes former Hampshire Bus coach-seated Bristol VRT 099 (NEL117P) in Kinnoull Street, Perth on 26 April 1991. (K.A.Jenkinson)

Yeowart fleet. In East Sussex, Hastings Bristol VRT 517 suffered roof damage after attempting to pass under the low bridge in Sackville Road, Bexhill on 5 November and as a replacement, a VRT was transferred from Hampshire Bus five days later. From this same source came 2 Leyland Nationals and in addition, Hastings received from Southdown a 1980 Leyland Leopard which had been fitted with a new Plaxton Paramount 3200 body in 1984. The Hampshire Bus fleet was the subject of several changes with 4 Robin Hood-bodied Iveco 49.10 minibuses, a Plaxton-bodied Leopard and 3 Plaxton Paramount-bodied Tiger coaches arriving from Southdown, and 2 Leyland Nationals and 5 Bristol VRTs being taken out of service. Also withdrawn was accident-damaged Bristol VRT 359 while a previous low bridge victim, Alexander-bodied Olympian 205 was returned to service following extensive repairs undertaken by Southdown at its Worthing depot. The flow of Bristol VRTs to Scotland continued when two were sent to Perth by East Midland, these replacing Stagecoach's last FS-type Lodekka and a Bristol FLF6G.

Before the end of the year, several more ex.Hong Kong Daimler CVG6s had reached Malawi, via Speedybus and the customary long sea voyage and overland route, to bring the total of this type in the African fleet to 57 and it was learned that these were to be joined by a further 13 during 1991. Also added to the Blantyre-based 'Cityline' fleet was a former Kowloon Motor Bus Metsec-bodied 102-seat, dual-

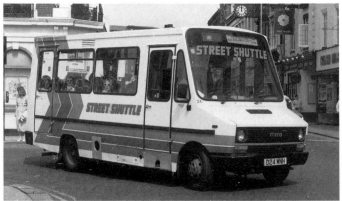

door low height Daimler Fleetline of 1974 vintage which had taken up its duties on 15 August and was Stagecoach Malawi's first rear engined double decker. By now, the fleet had grown to total no fewer than 364 buses and coaches

East Midland's former Magicbus three-axle Alexander-bodied Leyland Olympian was used to tour Britain in November 1990 as part of the BCC campaign 'Buses mean business'. Members of the public were invited to sign their names upon the bus which is seen here in Leeds Central Bus Station.

three-axle Olympian Megadekka was, in November, used for a nationwide tour to gain publicity for a Bus & Coach Council campaign which advocated the bus as a solution to urban congestion. Specially painted in an all-over white livery and carrying the legend 'Buses Mean Business', the public were invited to sign their names on the exterior of the bus to demonstrate their support.

In a determined attempt to retaliate against the growing number of taxis plying for hire in Corby and attract passengers back to the buses, United Counties who already operated their 'Street Shuttle' minibuses in the town, on 12 November launched a new service under the title 'Corby's Magic Minis'. Using 8 former Ribble Robin Hood-bodied Iveco 49.10s, all of which were painted in a striking new livery of black with gold Stagecoach-style stripes and chevrons and had their seating reduced from 18 to 13 to increase the space available for shopping and baby buggies etc. in special racks, the new service operated at intervals of 3-5 minutes from 9.00am to 6.00pm on Mondays to Saturdays. Within weeks of its introduction, this new operation was proving most successful, rolling together the very best features of a taxi with all the convenience of a regular minibus service at prices passengers could afford.

At the start of December, Hastings & District low bridge victim, Bristol VRT 517, had its roof repaired externally (but not internally) and began a new career as a driver training bus. One of Hastings' two Bristol LH6Ls, which had remained in store unused since their transfer from Hampshire Bus in September, was despatched to Perth to join the Stagecoach fleet on 13 December while during that same week, one of Magicbus's Perth Panther Alexander-bodied Mercedes 709D minibuses - G270GSL - visited the head office of every Stagecoach subsidiary in Britain to deliver stocks of the Group's 1991 calendar, a duty performed the previous year by one of the hired Devon General Ford Transit minibuses. Meanwhile, Southdown had applied Eastbourne & District fleet names to several of its Leyland Nationals following a service revision in the Eastbourne area under which full sized buses were needed on certain routes.

Having arranged three excursions to London's Christmas Lights on 1, 10 and 20 December, Hastings & District despatched its open-top Bristol VRT (570) to the capital to operate that end of the tour, those taking part travelling from Kent to London and back on one of the company's coaches in order to provide a high degree of comfort for the longest part of the journey. As the open-top double decker had by 19 December been returned to its winter store, it is thought that the third trip was not operated however. Continuing the Christmas theme, Hastings Leyland National no.1 (PTF753L) was suitably decorated and operated from 17 to 24 December with a Santa board attached to its front panel and was during this period, driven by staff dressed in Santa costume.

Despite having yet to notch up its first success in the Scottish Bus Group sell-off, Stagecoach Holdings had

comprising 14 Albion VK55s, 27 Dahmers, 68 Leyland Victory Mk.Is, 154 Leyland Victory Mk.2s, 26 ERF Trailblazers, 63 Daimler CVG6s, 1 Bristol FLF6G Lodekka, 1 Daimler Fleetline, 3 Leyland Tigers, 2 Leyland Leopards, 3 minicoaches and 2 driver training vehicles, whilst the total staff had been increased to 2,750 including 6 UK expatriots. Major improvements to servicing and maintenance facilities were being carried out at Mataka Road (Blantyre) and Lilongwe depots and discussions with several of the country's independent bus operators led to the start of franchising agreements wherby better co-ordinated timetables could be introduced for the benefit of Malawi's bus passengers. Due to increased passenger demands, the company applied for permission to operate a second weekly journey travelling through Zambia to Harare in Zimbabwe, and after this was granted, Stagecoach Malawi turned their attention to the possibility of starting a new service from Lilongwe to Dar-es-Salaam in Tanzania which, subject to approval being given by the Tanzanian Government, would be operated by new ERF vehicles.

Back home, further consolidation was achieved in Cumbria when, on 19 November, Cumberland Motor Services purchased the 3-coach business of Andy Vine, Cleator Moor, whose operations were mainly works and schools contracts and private hire. None of the three coaches - an AEC Reliance and two Leyland Leopards - were used by their new owner and were instead, immediately placed in store to await eventual disposal. Illustrating Stagecoach's continuing support for charity, one of Southdown's coach-seated NCME-bodied Volvo D10M double deckers toured Britain from 20 to 24 November in connection with the BBC's 'Children in Need' appeal. Additionally, East Midland's

One of United Counties ex.Ribble Robin Hood-bodied Iveco 49.10s - 303 (D726YBV) in its new black & gold 'Magic Minis' livery negotiates a road junction in a Corby housing estate soon after the introduction of this new operation in November 1990. (United Counties)

After spending several months in store since its acquisition from Wallace Arnold Tours of Leeds, Cumberland Plaxton Paramount-bodied Volvo 157 was given registration WVT618 transferred from a Southdown Leyland Tiger and, like its sisters, was painted into full Shearings livery for operation on that company's tours. It is seen here at Workington depot early in May 1991 before taking up its new duties. (Campbell Morrison)

submitted a bid for each of the subsidiaries which had to date been placed on the market. Surprisingly, in early December they decided not to bid for the troubled Kelvin Central company, and thus in the absence of any other bidders left the way clear for its management buy-out team to acquire it for a nominal sum. No reason was given for this sudden change of heart and it can only be assumed that after seeing Kelvin Central's problems, Stagecoach no longer felt that it was an attractive acquisition compared with the other SBG subsidiaries still to be privatised.

Having waited with bated breath for the Monopoly and Mergers Commission's report on their acquisition of Formia Ltd., when this was published on 20 December Stagecoach must have been relieved to find that although the report concluded that the merger might be expected to operate against public interest, it did not recommend the divestment of Hastings operations from Stagecoach as this would be likely to lead to one dominant supplier giving way to another, and would also risk disruption of services and inconvenience passengers while the change was being implemented. A number of measures were recommended which it was believed would be more effective in remedying the adverse effects of the merger. Before any glimmer of relief could be experienced however, the Secretary for Trade and Industry, Peter Lilley, announced that he rejected the MMC's findings and instructed the Office of Fair Trading to hold further talks with Stagecoach over the possibility of divesting part of the Hastings operation to stimulate competition in the area and to report back within two months. This led some observers to believe that the company were facing another Portsmouth situation and that they may now lose another part of their Southdown empire during the early months of 1991, despite

neither report actually recommending divestment.

By the start of 1991, Stagecoach International's activities in the Far East had grown considerably, with no fewer than 42 buses being operated in the Peoples' Republic of China. These comprised 1 Daimler CVG6LX/30, 19 Daimler CVG6LX/34, 14 former London 30ft. long Daimler Fleetlines and 8 33ft. long Fleetlines, all of which had been acquired from Kowloon Motor Bus Co. from whom Speedybus Enterprises had first refusal of all its surplus vehicles, the only condition being that these must be removed from Hong Kong within a reasonable period of time and must not be operated in the Crown Colony. As has been previously mentioned, before being despatched across the border to the Peoples' Republic, all 42 buses were rebuilt by Speedybus to make them suitable for left-hand boarding, and on the Daimler CVGs the entrance doors were repositioned (on the offside) at the centre and rear instead of the front and centre. This work completed, the buses were then repainted into their respective all-over advertising liveries (for Mild Seven, BIF Furniture, Winston, Weinsen or Ransonic), although six of the Fleetlines were surprisingly given Stagecoach corporate colours, and in this form were despatched across the border to take up their duties in several Chinese cities : Chengdu (1 CVG30, 5 CVG34s), Hangzhou (7 CVG6/34S), Wuzhou (2 CVG34s, 5 CRG30s, 1 CRG33), Fushan (2 CVG34s), Dalian (1 CVG34, 2 CRG30), Changchun (2 CVG34), Tianjin (6 CRG30, 6 CRG33) and Fuzhou (1 CRG30, 1 CRG33). Although it was wondered how the Chinese would cope with the maintenance of these buses in view of the difficulty of obtaining spares and the fact that most of their own vehicles were petrol rather than diesel engined, they have surprisingly proved to be extremely

One of Speedybus Enterprises' ex.Kowloon Motor Bus Co. Metsec-bodied Daimler CVG6s, rebuilt with its entrance door on the offside, is seen here followed by a single deck articulated trolleybus in the Peoples' Republic of China on 28 December 1990 wearing an all-over advertising livery for Mild Seven cigarettes. As may be seen, it carries a Leyland badge above its radiator grille, a feature common to most of Kowloon's CVG6s. (C.Lau)

adaptive and have encountered few problems which have needed Speedybus's expertise. In addition to the above, Speedybus Services Ltd. have supplied (under similar contracts), 10 CVGs, 6 CRG30s and 10 CRG33s - all ex Kowloon Motor Bus - to the Chinese cities of Guangzhou, Chongqing and Guilin.

After remaining in store at Cumberland's Barrow depot since their return from Inverness Traction earlier in the year, the future of the ten tri-axle Talbot Pullman minibuses had been the subject of much speculation and it thus came as something of a surprise when one of these vehicles was resurrected in December and despatched to East Midland for further service. After being repainted in Stagecoach corporate colours, it took up its duties in the Maun Minibuses fleet towards the end of the month. Less fortunate was Ribble 47, a former United Transport Buses Robin Hood-bodied Iveco 49.10 minibus which, receiving extensive damage as a result of colliding with a house in Bolton, was withdrawn for cannibalisation.

A further Leyland Lynx added to Cumberland's fleet was C544RAO which, after spending a period of four years under evaluation by Ribble, had languished for several months at Leyland's Workington factory where its original engine was replaced by a Cummins L10 unit. Allocated to its new owner's Barrow depot, it quickly settled down in service alongside Cumberland's four other buses of this type. Although the ex.Wallace Arnold Volvo coaches acquired in September had yet to enter service with their new owner, during December 1990 / January 1991 all were re-registered with cherished numbers transferred from Southdown and, having been converted from 48 to 50 seaters following the removal of their onboard toilets, they were surprisingly repainted into Shearings Holidays livery for use under contract by that company on holiday tours etc. during the 1991 summer season. Following the introduction of a new service by Urswick Minibuses from Ulverston to Moorgarth, Cumberland retaliated on 5 January by launching a new competitive service over the same route, numbering this 8

and operating it with a minibus from its Ulverston outstation. Meanwhile, Ribble vacated its rented accommodation in Preston bus station and moved its traffic office back to the company's headquarters at Frenchwood Avenue while in the south of England, Hampshire Bus closed its Botley outstation on the fifth day of the month. Hampshire Bus also evaluated a Wadham Stringer-bodied 35-seat Dennis Dart painted in Eastbourne Buses livery on several services in Winchester from 28 January to 5 February and in addition, examined a Dennis dart destined for Southampton CityBus, although this was not used in service during its one day stay.

January 1991 began with Hastings Buses imposing a total ban on smoking on all its buses from the opening day of the new year, a similar ban also being applied to those parts of Southdown where it had not previously been implemented and as a result, the whole of Stagecoach (South) - from Andover to Hastings - became 'smoke-free' from this date. A new coach holiday/minibreak brochure was produced for the 1991 season and this bore the names of both Hastings Coaches and Derwyn's Coach Tours, thus linking the two company's programmes. Hastings remaining Bristol LH6L which, like its sister had never been used since its arrival from Hampshire Bus, left its Kent home early in January to travel northwards to Perth where it had previously operated for a brief period in the autumn of 1989. Joining this bus were a trio of LH6Ls from Hampshire Bus which had likewise originated from East Midland, two having already seen service on Tayside for a few weeks some fourteen months earlier. These were quickly despatched onwards to join the Inverness Traction fleet where two were allocated to that company's Ardersier outstation, mainly for use on local contract duties. Also on the move was one of Southdown's Plaxton-bodied Leyland Leopard coaches which was transferred to the Hastings fleet while the ex.Kelvin Alexander-bodied Leopard which had latterly served as a uniform store at Stagecoach's Inveralmond depot, Perth was sold for scrap after being replaced by yet another portacabin.

A surprise move in Winchester saw Hampshire Bus introduce two new minibus services numbered 24/25 from the City Centre to Oliver's Battery and cross-city from Winnall to Oliver's battery. Commencing on 7 January, these services were marketed under the Stagecoach title and the vehicles allocated for their operation were given Stagecoach fleet names. Ironically, one of the first vehicles to receive its new identity was Robin Hood-bodied Iveco 49.10 F22PSL which had started its life in Stagecoach's Perth Panther fleet in July 1989 and was transferred to Southdown in February 1990 before moving to Hampshire Bus in January 1991. The decision to brand the new Winchester minibus services with the Stagecoach name was taken in the hope that Winchester would be chosen as a Bus & Coach Council 'Buses Mean Business' project which would result in significant publicity and thus reflect the Stagecoach Group's dedication to the improvement and wider use of bus travel throughout Britain. Although Hampshire Bus do not intend to extend the use of the Stagecoach name on a general basis, it will probably be used for any further minibus conversions in the Winchester area in the future.

January 7 witnessed a number of changes to the service network in Inverness. Among these was the re-routeing of service 3 to run from the town centre to Kinmylies instead of Milton Crescent; the withdrawal of service 6 from the town centre to Ardness and the addition of an evening service on route 4C from the town centre to Kinmylies with one journey extended to Craig Dunain Hospital. More importantly, an hourly service was introduced on Sundays on routes 4C and 5, this being the first time that Inverness Traction had operated on the Sabbath. Despite these changes, Stagecoach found itself facing the possibility of yet another investigation by the Office of Fair Trading following allegations by the Highland Regional Council of route-sharing between Inverness Traction and Highland Scottish which effectively ended competition in the town. Although obviously not welcoming a further OFT investigation, both companies were confident that in the event of the Council's complaint being taken on board, the final result would absolve them of any malpractice.

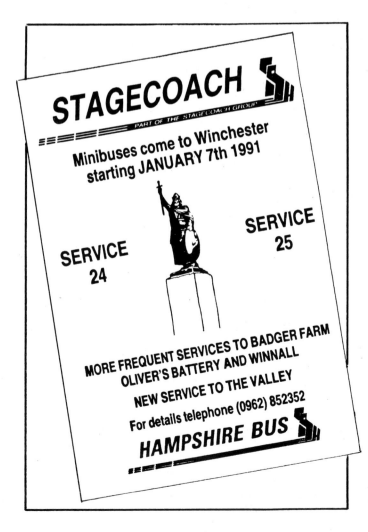

STAGECOACH
PART OF THE STAGECOACH GROUP

Minibuses come to Winchester
starting JANUARY 7th 1991

SERVICE
24

SERVICE
25

MORE FREQUENT SERVICES TO BADGER FARM
OLIVER'S BATTERY AND WINNALL

NEW SERVICE TO THE VALLEY

For details telephone (0962) 852352

HAMPSHIRE BUS

SOUTHERN DIVESTMENT

The long-running saga of Stagecoach's Portsmouth operations was eventually resolved on 18 January when the company finalised the sale of Southdown Portsmouth to its old adversary, Harry Blundred's Transit Holdings. This resulted in the divestment of all the company's services operating between Portsmouth, Waterlooville and Petersfield and those to Porchester, Paulsgrove and on Portsea Island. Also included in the deal were the routes between Portsmouth and Fareham, and Havant and Fareham and the former Citybus depot at Highland Road, Eastney. This was to be used by Transit Holdings until the expiry of its lease in May, after which the Transit fleet was to be moved to the old Southdown premises at Hilsea West which was then to be reopened. Hilsea East, despite also being part of the deal, will not echo again to the sound of buses however, due to it being too derelict to re-occupy. Following the Portsmouth sale, Southdown retained 30 peak vehicles operating in the Havant area and from Havant to Portsmouth and Waterlooville, stabling these at Havant and Leigh Park with maintenance being carried out at Chichester.

Transit assumed responsibility for its new territory on 20 January when a total of 104 buses and coaches along with 5 ancillary vehicles were transferred from Stagecoach Holdings to the newly-formed Portsmouth Transit. These comprised 26 Leyland Nationals, 33 Alexander-bodied Atlanteans, 12 East Lancs-bodied Atlanteans, 19 Robin Hood-bodied Iveco 49.10 minibuses and 9 Leyland Nationals from Hastings Buses. In addition to these, 11 Leyland Nationals, 2 Leopard coaches and 14 Dodge minibuses were tempoarily loaned to Transit by Southdown and it was rumoured that some of the latter may eventually be purchased and thus remain in Portsmouth, although a number of the Leyland Nationals were returned to their rightful owner during the following two weeks, some being immediately transferred onwards to Hastings Buses. Prior to finalising the sale of Southdown Portsmouth, the company had transferred all its Bristol VRTs, Leyland National 2s, its eight 'Stagecoach standard' Alexander-bodied Olympians and two NCME-bodied Volvo D10Ms to Havant bus station or Leigh Park on 1 December 1990 for continued use on the handful of services which were to be retained in the Portsmouth area.

Although no longer part of the Stagecoach story, it is nevertheless of interest to see that with effect from 20 January, Transit Holdings applied vinyls to all its acquired vehicles to publicise their new identity. New fleet names 'Portsmouth Transit'; 'Red Admiral' (for country services) and 'Blue Admiral' (for city services) were used and joining

Southdown Bristol VRT 649 in an all-over advertising livery awaits its passengers at Portsmouth in April 1991 whilst adorned with 'Top Ten Bus' vinyls in its upper deck bulkhead window and above the cab side window. (Travelscene)

the 'acquired' fleet were four Ford Transit minibuses from the now defunct Docklands Transit operation. The liveries in which the new Portsmouth Transit fleet commenced operations were extremely varied and ranged from Stagecoach corporate colours to Hastings blue cream & yellow, Southdown apple green & cream, Red Admiral red & black, Top Line yellow & black, Portsmouth Citybus ivory & red and plain white with blue wheels, whilst a couple retained their all-over advertising liveries. This hue of colour continued to expand as more minibuses from Bay Line and Transit Holding's other fleets were drafted into Portsmouth as replacements for conventional-sized buses. Except for Southdown's Senior Traveller's half-fare passes which were to continue to be valid until May when new, cheaper half-fare passes were to be introduced, the interavailability of tickets with Southdown ceased on 10 February. On this date, the Stagecoach-owned company launched a new multi-journey ticket in the Havant area which was marketed under the title 'Top Ten' and was confined to use on Southdown buses. In order to publicise this and identify the company's buses amongst the plethora of liveries associated with Transit, all Southdown's buses operating in the area were adorned with 'Top Ten Bus' vinyls placed in or near their destination screens and on each side of the bodywork. Although this practise was to continue for some time, it became less important as Transit's conversion to 100% minibus operation was completed. Additionally, Southdown put into action a priority painting scheme under which concentration was given to the transformation of all its Havant and Leigh Park-based buses into Stagecoach corporate colours.

In addition to the major exodus from Southdown's subsidiary fleets shown above, open-top Leyland Atlantean 11 (ERV251D) was transferred to Cumberland Motor Services where it was to be painted into the old Southdown-style apple green & cream livery for use on services in the Lake District. In the opposite direction, Magicbus's solitary

Still wearing Stagecoach corporate livery in April 1991, Alexander-bodied Atlantean UOR332T despite displaying its new Portsmouth Transit fleet names above its destination screen and below the cab side window, continues to carry its old Southdown Portsmouth name and Stagecoach Holdings logo below its windscreens. (Travelscene)

Although Stagecoach were operating buses in the Peoples' Republic of China, Cumberland 1480, an ECW-bodied Leyland Atlantean still wearing NBC poppy red livery and Carlislebus fleet name - complete with NBC 'double N' logos - was not destined to travel to the Far East despite the wording on its side poster ! (K.A.Jenkinson)

B-series Leyland National was removed from the reserve fleet at Spittalfield and sent to Hastings & District for further service, the latter also receiving a number of Leyland Nationals from Southdown including the six ex.Portsmouth National 2s. Some of the latter were placed in service still in their original owner's colours with their Citybus fleet name painted out and a Hastings Buses name added across the front. Completing the reshuffle was Southdown's Robin Hood-bodied Iveco minibus 926 which was sent to Hampshire Bus in exchange for its sister, 925. Following its fleet rationalisation, Southdown together with Hastings & District and Hampshire Bus collectively advertised no less than 37 surplus vehicles for sale in mid-January. These comprised 15 Alexander-bodied Atlanteans, 3 former Citybus open-top Atlanteans, 3 Bristol RELLs, 6 Freight Rover Sherpas, 7 Dodge S56 minibuses, the unique Wright-bodied Dodge with double rear doors for a tail lift, a Bristol FLF6B driver trainer and an ex. Citybus Leyand PD2 training vehicle. North of the border, Magicbus further reduced its reserve fleet of Leyland Nationals during January 1991 with the sale of 10 to Lister (dealer) of Bolton, Lancashire, whilst also leaving Scotland was an Inverness Traction Alexander-bodied Mercedes minibus which was transferred to Cumberland and two of the East Lancs-bodied Dodge S56 minibuses previously used as the staff shuttle and tea bus at

Perth which were sold to Preston Borough Transport. The latter were required for use on the Lancashire County Council contracted Park and Ride service in Preston which Borough Transport had gained from Ribble on 28 January. In order to provide replacements for the two Dodge S56s, a pair of Ribble's ex.Mercers of Grimsargh Dormobile-bodied Ford Transits were removed from store and despatched to Perth where they took up their new duties at the end of the month. One of these buses wore an all-over advertising livery for St.George's Shopping Centre, Preston while the other still sported its Badgerline livery which it had retained throughout its period of operation with Mercers !

Criticisms were levelled at Stagecoach Holdings by one of Cumbria's Labour Members of Parliament, Dale Campbell Savours who tabled a question to the Parliamentary Committee of Public Accounts asking what bus stations and property had been included in the valuation of Cumberland Motor Services upon its sale by the National Bus Company in July 1987. When civil servants were unable to provide an answer, the MP accused them of deliberately denying him access to the information and continued by stating that Keswick bus station had already been sold for redevelopment for £705,000, that some spare land at Workington was currently being disposed of and that the same could soon be applied to Cumberland's premises in Carlisle. The Workington land was in fact not sold until March 1991 when its ownership passed to William Low whilst at Carlisle, the bus station at Lowther Street was being redeveloped to include new terminal facilities. Adding to his string of inaccuracies, he said that the Department of Transport had been conned and that many of his constituents were extremely angry, especially in Maryport where the alternative site chosen for a bus station is now a bus stop with a shed outside someone's house, and asked why there had been no clawback so that profits from such sales could be returned to the taxpayer. In reality, Maryport bus station had been closed by the NBC ! The MP made further comments regarding the future of Whitehaven bus station, but these again proved to be completely unfounded and when the terminal building was closed on 15 February, it was merely to allow it to be re-roofed and generally refurbished. During the three months that it was out of use, all the services normally terminating within its confines were transferred to outside stops in Tangier Street where additional shelters had been erected. Unfortunately however, the new stops were often blocked by local taxis and in an attempt to prevent them from hampering the buses using these new, temporary picking up points, Cumberland judiciously parked one of its Reeve Burgess-bodied Mercedes minibuses (46 - D46UAO) in Tangier Street for this purpose. As far as Keswick was concerned, the new

Used by Stagecoach for staff taxi duties at Inveralmond depot, Perth, Freight Rover Sherpa D572EWS was acquired from Ribble early in 1991. Despite still painted in Badgerline livery, this bus was used by Mercers of Grimsargh before passing to Ribble and still carries a Mercers name vinyl in the window behind the cab door. (K.A.Jenkinson)

One of Cumberland's Alexander-bodied Leyland Tiger coaches, 643 (WAO643Y) rests in the yard of Little Broughton outstation between its school contract duties in April 1991. (B.K.Pritchard)

redeveloped bus station was brought into use on 17 March, thus marking the start of a new chapter in the provision of bus services in this Lakeland town.

Seeing the difficulties facing Tayside Public Transport Co. Ltd. which had for some months been he subject of a possible management / employees buy-out and following the dispensation by the undertaking of three of its senior managers in an attempt to tackle its projected £1 million trading shortfall, Stagecoach contacted the Scottish Office with a bid for the Tayside undertaking. If successful, this would give the company a major foothold in an area where it had not previously had a major presence and would compensate for it being advised not to bid for Strathtay Scottish in order to avoid further interest by the Monopolies & Mergers Commission. Interest was however shown in Fife Scottish which was placed on the market during the early spring of 1991, this company being adjacent to Magicbus' Tayside operations but far enough away to not be considered to be creating a monopoly situation.

During February, Stagecoach acquired a further two Bristol VRTs for cannibalisation, one coming from United Counties, the other from East Midland. Immediately taken to the Spittalfield graveyard, they replaced the previous provider of spare parts - ex.United Counties ANV776J - which was sold to Dunsmore (breaker) of Larkhall for scrap. More re-registrations took place early in the year after another Routemaster donated its number to one of the company's Duple-bodied Volvo coaches while some of the ex.Cumberland Leopards were re-registered yet again, their cherished marks being transferred to more of the Volvo coaches. In England, East Midland gained two Leyland Nationals from Hastings Buses on 7 February and during the following month, Cumberland added yet another Inverness Traction Alexander-bodied Mercedes 709D to its ever growing fleet of this type of minibus. In an attempt to warn drivers of full-height double deckers which would not pass beneath Sackville Arch, Bexhill, Hastings Buses fitted some of its Bristol VRTs of such dimensions with red steering wheels whilst others were given red spokes to their conventional black wheels. Later, on 25 February, Southdown loaned one of its Plaxton-bodied Leopards to Southampton CityBus to assist them with their current coaching requirements.

Early in March, another convertible open-top Bristol VRT was transferred from Southdown to Scotland and, along with its sister which had moved northwards in June 1990, it was repainted into a new version of the Group's corporate livery which omitted the chevrons at the rear. Upon completion, both buses were then despatched to Inverness where they were to be used on a new open-top summer service. Back in

Perth, although the Perth Panther name continued to be used on Stagecoach's publicity material and timetables, it no longer appeared on the vehicles themselves and the remaining four Leyland Nationals still in service now carried Stagecoach fleet names. Although still occasionally appearing on Perth city services, the Nationals were also used on a variety of other duties around Perth and Spittalfield and were even sometimes used on the company's longer services such as that to Pitlochry. About to leave the fleet was Bristol LD5G Lodekka OVL473 which, having never been used in service since its acquisition in October 1986, was surprisingly given a heavy dock and, after gaining a Class V MOT test certificate, was offered for sale still wearing the faded light blue livery in which it had arrived some five years earlier. Before its departure, it was however reregistered LDS448A, its original number being transferred to ex.Cumberland Leopard 191.

Meanwhile, overseas developments continued to feature in the news with the Group's Canadian Gray Coach Lines operations undergoing a number of significant changes. Amongst these are the sale in April to the Ontario Northland Transportation Commission of their northern routes to North Bay and Sudbury and the return of most of the former employees to the Toronto Transit Commission. In order to bypass the former pool arrangements with U.S.Greyhound Lines Inc. because of labour problems on their services in the USA, Gray Coach made pooling arrangements with American carriers, Empire Trailways and Adirondack Trailways on a through service between Toronto and New York City via Buffalo, with an additional through coach between Toronto, Buffalo and Rochester. So popular has this new service proved that that on the 9.00pm departure from Toronto on the Thursday before Easter, no fewer than nine coaches were needed to accommodate all those wishing to travel ! Following the success of this new service, another pooled route has been started between Toronto, Buffalo and Washington D.C., this being operated in partnership with Empire Trailways and Capitol Trailways. In a further attempt to expand their operations, Gray Coach Lines are also examining a number of dormant route licences in southern Ontario in what is known as the Golden Triangle surrounding Toronto, some of which, if taken up, would act as feeder services into the Government of Ontario's commuter rail network.

Having held the famous Gray Line sightseeing franchise for the round Toronto and Niagara Falls conducted sightseeing tours for many years, these have now been remodelled in conjunction with local operator, Toronto Tours Ltd. For 1991, the previous six separate sightseeing destinations have been

Painted in an all-white livery, East Midland's ex.Maun Optare-bodied Leyland Cub C807KBT stands out of use at Sutton Junction depot in June 1991. (K.A.Jenkinson)

Freshly repainted in all-white livery and awaiting its Stagecoach stripes and chevrons, East Midland B-series Leyland National 612 stands in the yard of Sutton Junction depot in August 1990. (P.French)

developed into one 'value for money' round Toronto coach
tour which although normally operated by Gray Coach's MCI
coaches, may soon also be worked by the former
Stagecoach Bristol FLF6G Lodekka (BHU976C) converted to
open-top configuration by East Midland. Should this prove
impracticable, the Lodekka will instead be employed as a
promotional and sales vehicle. Remaining on the vintage
theme, Gray Coach Lines also operates a 'Vintage Streetcar
Tour' of Toronto using the sleek PCC single deck trams of
the Toronto Transit Commission.

Across the world in Africa, Stagecoach Malawi, who were
experiencing operational difficulties with their Leyland Tiger
coaches which were fast becoming unreliable and costly to
maintain, acquired four former Parks of Hamilton three
year-old Plaxton Paramount 3500-bodied Volvo B10Ms as
replacements. Painted into Stagecoach's corporate colours
before leaving Britain, these coaches with their air

conditioning, toilet and food/drink servery will provide
Coachline with up-market vehicles for their long distance
international services and will undoubtedly assist them in
further establishing new areas of operation in the future.

SUCCESS IN THE FAR NORTH

After unsuccessfully submitting bids for most of the
Scottish Bus Group subsidiaries, Stagecoach Holdings finally
achieved their aim on 27 March when they acquired Northern
Scottish Omnibuses Ltd., beating Northern's management
buy-out team, and the other bidders, Go Ahead Northern and
Drawlane. The Aberdeen-based company had been on the
market since October 1990, the decision on its future having
been delayed while the Scottish Transport Group took advice
on the Monopolies and Mergers Commisision attitude to a
possible bid from Grampian Transport. Adding a further 206
vehicles to its Scottish-based fleet, the acquisition of
Bluebird Northern gave Stagecoach a major foothold in an
area where, except for its express services prior to their sale
to Caledonian Express, it had never had a presence.

Stagecoach were particularly delighted with their success
as Bluebird's fleet which comprised mainly Leyland
Olympians, Leopards, Nationals and Tigers was compatible
with its own corporate fleet and thus allowed vehicles to be
interchanged whenever the need arose. Within two days of
gaining control, Stagecoach's corporate livery made its
appearance when Alexander-bodied Leyland Olympian LO69
emerged from the paint shops at Aberdeen in its new colours
to which traditional-style Bluebird fleet names and logos had
been added. Following the immediate resignation of
Northern's managing director, John Westaby, Neil Renilson

was appointed to this position in addition to retaining his
existing duties. Although Highland Scottish, the final SBG
subsidiary to be offered for sale, was placed on the market in
March, it was thought unlikely that Stagecoach would submit
a bid in view of its Inverness Traction operation being in the
heart of Highland's territory, thus possibly creating a
monopoly situation which would quickly be put under
investigation.

On the same day that Bluebird Northern became a member of the Stagecoach Group, a further reshuffle of vehicles took place when Ribble transferred its semi-preserved Leyland PD3/5 (TCK841) and driver training Leyland PD2/13 (ABV784A, originally HRN32) to Cumberland Motor Services who were to use both buses on driver tuition duties. Prior to this, Cumberland's nine remaining tri-axle Talbot Pullman minibuses had been removed from store at Barrow between 1 and 15 March and despatched to East Midland to join the other bus of this type which had departed to Chesterfield in December of the previous year. After being repainted into corporate livery, some of these were given East Midland fleet names while the remainder were lettered for Mansfield & District.

Continuing its tidying-up process, on 5 March 1991 a new company was formed under the title of Stagecoach Scotland Ltd. This took over all the Group's activities in Inverness, Tayside and Strathclyde and unlike Stagecoach South and North West, the legal lettering on all the Scottish-based vehicles was altered to reflect the new company, although the trading names such as Magicbus and IT (Inverness Traction) continued to be used as fleet names on the Glasgow and Inverness-based vehicles. By now, Southdown and Hastings & District had been placed under the control of Stagecoach South, leaving only East Midland not included in any of the three regional companies.

In addition to preparing its open-top apple-green & cream liveried Bristol VRTs and Atlanteans for their re-entry into

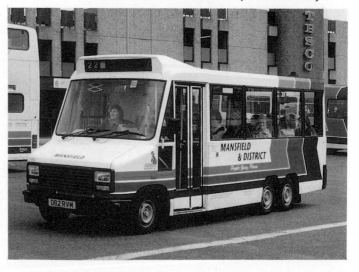

service for their summer duties on the Lakeland Experience operation from Bowness to Ambleside in conjunction with the Windermere Iron Steamboat Company, Cumberland also repainted three of its Reeve Burgess-bodied Mercedes L608D minibuses into this same livery. These were to be used on the new Lakeland Experience 'Coniston Rambler' service from Bowness to Coniston via Windermere and Ambleside. Another Cumberland mini to gain a livery change was coach-seated Robin Hood-bodied Iveco 49.10 80 (D217NUR) which appeared in the company's yellow & tan Coachline colours.

On the first day of April, Cumberland began operations on a new Social Services contract in Barrow in Furness, ferrying people from the Dalton and Barrow areas to Mill Lane Old People's Home on Walney Island and for this purpose, reinstated one of its withdrawn ex.Yeowarts Reeve Burgess-bodied Mercedes 608D minibuses. On the following day, Ribble applied a smoking ban on all its buses, thus continuing Stagecoach's smokeless travel policy while at the other end of the country, Hastings Coaches produced a continental excursion brochure for the period June to August 1991. Similarly, Shirebrook-based Midland Travel also launched two new excursion brochures, one of which offered weekend breaks to 32 different destinations between April and November, all at the amazingly low price of £32. Midland Travel's other brochure publicised the company's express services to a variety of British coastal resorts and a wide range of day and evening excursions. Amongst these were a number of evening trips advertised as being undertaken on a 30-year old vintage London double decker, and although the company's fleet included several Routemasters, two

privately-owned buses of this type - immaculately restored RM10 and front entrance ex.Northern General FPT603C painted in London General livery - were also available for use if required. In order to further develop and expand their

business, Midland Travel launched an exclusive Midland Travelclub to which membership was available for an annual subscription of £10. Amongst the benefits members received was forward information on holidays etc., and so successful was this venture, that within ten days of its launch, some 1600 members had already been enrolled.

Another innovative move by East Midland was the monthly publication of 'Passenger News', a series of A5-size leaflets which were aimed at keeping passengers informed of service changes and time table leaflets which were available. In conjunction with Drawlane subsidiary, C-Line and the Countryside Commission, East Midland were also involved in the operation of a number of summer Sunday day tours of the Peak District from May to September, thus providing the opportunity to view the scenic beauty of this area in a more relaxed manner than by using a private car. On the debit side, East Midland lost some 4% profitable turnover as a result of the massive cuts made by South Yorkshire PTE to contracted services and as a result, the company had to revise a number of its duties during April.

Following the success of its Magic Minis in Corby, United Counties started a second route in the town on 2 April which it believes will be equally well patronised. Further north, Inverness Traction revised some of its services towards the end of the month including the replacement of route 8 by an extension of the 12 and the extension of services 16/17 from Fort George and Croy respectively to Nairn to form a circular service which is to be promoted as a 'Tourist Trail' taking in Castle Stuart, Fort George, Cawdor Castle and Culloden Battlefield and upon which the two open-top Bristol VRTs are to be employed. On the vehicle front, one of United Counties Routemasters (705 - 68CLT) was re-registered ABD892A, this being the first of that subsidiary's buses of that type to be thus transformed.

Soon after control of Bluebird Northern passed to Stagecoach Holdings Ltd., the former SBG company, in April, acquired the Aberdeen to Banchory stage carriage service of F. & M. Clark of Banchory together with three Leyland Leopards - two Alexander bus-bodied examples which had begun life with Alexander Northern, and a Plaxton coach-bodied variant, all of which were quickly sold by the Stagecoach Group without giving further service. Following this sale, Clark's Taxis & Coaches continued to operate its other stage services and several schools contracts without change from its established premises at Dykehead Garage, Banchory. At the other end of the country, Southdown moved its head office from Walwers Lane, Lewes to Lewes Enterprise Centre.

On 15 April, Stagecoach's Tayside services underwent minor revision with one or two additional early morning and evening journeys being added to a few routes and revised times being applied to others. The Spittalfield - Blairgowrie services 12 & 13 which had previously run on Tuesdays,

With a 'School Bus' board in its windscreen, East Midland 411 (TSU642W), an Alexander-bodied Leyland Leopard acquired from Maun, Mansfield looks smart in its Stagecoach corporate livery as it passes through Retford bus station in June 1991. (K.A.Jenkinson)

Wednesdays and Saturdays lost their Wednesday operation, and on Sundays, Perth city service 7 from Hillend to Scone was reduced from a half-hourly to an hourly frequency. More surprising however was the introduction of 'hail and ride' facilities on route 7 in the New Scone area, as this service was usually maintained by double deckers, a type not often

Above : Delicensed awaiting recertification at Spittalfield in April 1991 is 098 (YTU358S), a former East Midland Bristol VRT which has gained the as-yet unrepainted front panel from United Counties 836, a VRT acquired by Stagecoach for cannibalisation. (K.A.Jenkinson)

Left : Turning into Mill Street from Kinnoull Street, Perth whilst operating city service 10 on 26 April 1991 is 252 (G252TSL), an Alexander-bodied Mercedes 709D which, as can be seen, carries advertising on its side panels for Perth's Leisure Pool. (K.A.Jenkinson)

Still carrying an Inverness advert on its side panels and an 'IT' logo on its bonnet, Inverness Traction Alexander-bodied Mercedes 709D 292 (G292TSL) is seen here at Stagecoach's Inveralmond depot, Perth on 6 April 1991 whilst being used on staff taxi duties. Later in that month, 292 was, together with two other Mercedes 709Ds, transferred to Bluebird Northern for further service. (K.A.Jenkinson)

Passing Stagecoach Holdings headquarters in Charlotte Street, Perth on 26 April 1991 is former Bluebird Northern ECW-bodied Leyland Olympian 032 (TSO32X) which on that occasion was being used on Perth city service 7 to Hillend. (K.A.Jenkinson)

associated with 'stop anywhere' operations. At around this same time, one of the two Perth-based ex.Ribble Freight Rover Sherpas was sold and was replaced by the sole remaining ex.Ribble/Barrow East Lancs-bodied Dodge S56 minibus which had been used in a non-PSV role in Inverness. Upon its arrival at Perth, it was put to use as the 'tea bus' at Mill Street where it has become a familiar sight in its all-white livery. As was to be expected, the movement of recently-acquired Bluebird Northern buses began within days

Standing at Stagecoach's Inveralmond depot, Perth on 26 April 1991 are Alexander-bodied Mercedes 709D minibus 254 (G254TSL) and ex.Barrow East Lancs-bodied Dodge S56 352 (D457BEO) which is usually used as the staff 'tea bus' at Mill Street, Perth. (K.A.Jenkinson)

of the company's transfer from the SBG to Stagecoach and after a handful had been witnessed travelling in a southerly direction along the M6 motorway, a pair of ECW-bodied Olympians were moved to Perth. Freshly repainted in Stagecoach's corporate livery, these were immediately put to use by Perth depot, mainly on city services, although one of the pair was unfortunatly damaged in an accident within days of entering service in its new adopted home and as a result spent a period of time under repair before reappearing in the city. Moving in the opposite direction were a Stagecoach Bristol VRT (URB160S) and an Alexander-bodied Mercedes minibus (G270TSL) which were 'sold' to Bluebird Northern together with two of Inverness Traction's Mercedes minis (G291/2TSL), these being allocated to McDuff, Elgin, Fraserburgh and Stonehaven depots respectively. Prior to its transfer to Bluebird, G292TSL had spent a brief period at Perth where it was employed mainly on staff taxi duties. Earlier in the month, one of the privately-owned ex.Glasgow Corporation double deckers which had been borrowed by Magicbus at Christmas 1989 returned once again to its native city when it was used for a few days by Magicbus on a temporary rail replacement service. At the other end of Stagecoach's territory, Hastings Plaxton-bodied Leyland Tiger coach 1001 (410DCD) was, during early April, given Derwyn's Coach Tours fleet names above its front wheel arch on both sides for use on tours and minibreaks organised jointly between the two companies.

As part of its continuing rationalisation plans, Ribble closed its Fleetwood depot on 27 April with the unfortunate loss of 30 jobs. Despite its full-sized buses being transferred to other depots, the company still maintained a presence in the town and following the closure of its depot in Birch Street, its 12 minibuses were housed at a site at Fleetwood Docks.

Despite the Routemaster fleet north of the border having been gradually reduced over the past three years and many of the examples withdrawn from service being used as a source of spares before being ultimately sold, during 1990 a quantity of spares were purchased from a Carlton breaker to enhance the stocks held at Stagecoach's Spittalfield premises. Included amongst these were numerous body parts including front wings, bonnets, cab doors and windows, plus of course a quantity of mechanical parts. Whether or not Stagecoach, East Midlands and United Counties

Left : One of 100 Alexander-bodied Mercedes Benz 709D minibuses purchased by Stagecoach Holdings for allocation to its various operating companies, G571PRM was placed in service by Ribble in June 1990. In Stagecoach corporate livery and carrying Zippy fleet names, it stands in Preston bus station on 9 September 1990. (J.Whitmore)

Left : With its new-style Ribble fleet name and Stagecoach Holdings logo positioned above its door, 416, one of the company's oldest Leyland Nationals, appears to be in excellent condition as it rests in the yard of Clitheroe depot on 11 May 1991. (K.A.Jenkinson)

Below left : United Counties Routemaster WLT908 complete with no smoking posters to each side of its front destination screen leaves no doubt as to its type with its Routemaster fleet names in several positions. (J.Whitmore)

Below : Some of the Routemaster spares - including the bonnet from ex.London Buses RM2176 - purchased by Stagecoach from a Carlton breaker in 1990 lie amongst the grass at Spittalfield depot in April 1991. (K.A.Jenkinson)

Amongst the Bristol VRTs in the fleet of East Midland are eight fitted with full-height ECW bodywork. One of these, 1201, leaves Mansfield bus station on 3 June 1991 whilst operating on Mansfield & District route 16 to Clipstone, a service ususlly maintained by Routemasters. In true East Midland fashion, its fleet name is placed below the lower deck windows rather than in the more customary Stagecoach Group position above the door.   (K.A.Jenkinson)

Freshly repainted in Stagecoach corporate colours and caught by the camera at Basingstoke in August 1989 is Hampshire Bus Bristol VRT 372 (RJT157R). (Ian Buck)

Right : Still in NBC poppy red & white livery and carrying pre-Stagecoach style Ribble fleet names, full height ECW-bodied Atlantean 1406 stands alongside corporate liveried Alexander-bodied Olympian 2183 at Morecambe depot on 22 August 1990. (K.A.Jenkinson)

Below : Approaching the bus station at The Hard, Portsmouth in July 1990 is Southdown Bristol VRT 686 which carries a 'cigar-band' advert for Jersey Royal potatoes and sports an electronic front destination display which is fitted off-centre.   (T.G.Walker)

Routemasters will survive long enough to use all this array of ex.London equipment is a matter of speculation, but with the mass of spares accumulated, it would seem possible that some buses of this type might enjoy many more days of service before their final departure from the Group's combined fleet.

Pledging their support to the Bus & Coach Council's 'Buses Mean Business' campaign, in addition to providing its Leyland Olympian Megadekka for a campaign tour of part of Britain in November 1990, the Stagecoach Group have worked closely with the BCC in several other directions. Joining discussions with the County Council in Northamptonshire, United Counties have proposed several ideas including the development of Bus Only lanes and green routes, new Park and Ride schemes and improvements to roadside facilities and in Bedford have suggested ways of enhancing bus operation in order to reduce the growing traffic congestion in the town. Ribble have joined in discussions centred around a green route in Preston and a Park and Ride scheme in Lancaster while East Midland have put forward a comprehensive scheme to create a green route for all buses over roads within the ring road scheme at

Mansfield. Hampshire Bus, as mentioned previously, have launched a new minibus scheme in Winchester and proposed plans to relieve pressure on the Southgate/High Street junction as well as suggesting a Park and Ride scheme which would assist in the reduction of growing traffic congestion in the city. Seeing the way ahead being in closer co-operation with local authorites, the Stagecoach Group appreciates that unless action is taken to reduce traffic in many areas, by the end of the century traffic will have almost ground to a halt - a situation which will be to the benefit of no-one.

Returning to Stagecoach's operational activities, Cumberland Motor Services suffered a blow when the Copeland Borough Council turned down a planning application for the company's Whitehaven depot to be relocated at a new site in the town at Red Lonning. As the company's parking area and vehicle wash adjacent to the railway station are soon to be vacated for redevelopment, the depot is now effectively homeless and an urgent search is underway to find an alternative site which will gain the approval of the local authority.

Having themselves withdrawn from the bidding for Strathtay Scottish following advise from the Office of Fair

Trading, Stagecoach waited eagerly to see who would emerge as the successful party. The announcement made in May showed that Strathtay's management had failed in their attempt to purchase their own company which instead had been gained by Barnsley-based Yorkshire Traction. Although Traction's chairman stated that he did not anticipate the need to make major changes at Strathtay, Stagecoach viewed this with some scepticism, especially as it appeared that the management/employee buy-out of Dundee-based Tayside Public Transport was expected to be drawn to a successful conclusion within the near future. Although there was as yet little competition in the Dundee area, the emergence of two 'new' operators could well spark a new bus war in the city and its surrounds, and should this occur, then Stagecoach might well feel that they are able to gain a larger slice of the action than they presently enjoy. This of course is, at the present time, merely speculation - only the fullness of time will confirm such possibilities . . . .

As had been expected, further rationalisation between Stagecoach's Scottish fleets took place towards the end of May when, following the successful transfer of one of Stagecoach's Bristol VRTs to Bluebird Northern during the previous month, a further two ex.East Midland buses of this type were despatched northwards in exchange for a pair of Bluebird's ECW-bodied Leyland Olympians which were immediately placed in service at Perth. More surprising however was the movement of one of Stagecoach's Leyland Nationals - 211 (GFX975N) from Spittalfield to Inverness, this being the first occasion that a vehicle of this type had operated in the Inverness Traction fleet while the four remaining Nationals, although licensed, were held at

Spittalfield as 'spare' vehicles. 402 (449CLT), a Plaxton-bodied Volvo coach which had been prepared for sale and painted into an all-white livery found a buyer at the ADT auction at Manchester, still fitted with its 'Routemaster' registration number.

Operationally, at the start of June, Bluebird Northern withdrew the majority of its city services in Aberdeen, this move being somewhat surprising in view of the fact that when part of the SBG, Bluebird had spent four years aggressively building these up. Withdrawn completely was the service from Heathryfold to Northfield whilst the 55 from Balnagask to Springhill was cut in half and the Torry to Northfield service was curtailed. Feeling obliged to fill the gaps left by Bluebird, Grampian Regional Transport quickly withdrew its rural services 7, 29, 30, 35, 63 and 67 in order to switch resources to the city area, thus leaving the Stagecoach-owned company to pick up what they wanted in the Balgownie, Inverurie and Banchory areas.

NOTHING VENTURED, NOTHING GAINED

Following their success in the acquisition of Bluebird Northern in March, Stagecoach were delighted to learn on 29 May that they had been given preferred bidder status for Fife Scottish whose headquarters were across the Tay at Kirkcaldy. Only hours before the announcement was made by the Scottish Office, a group of local Central Fife Members of Parliament who had learned of this, protested vigourously at the decision and immediately demanded that reconsideration be given to the bid submitted by the management and employees of the SBG subsidiary. As a result, the unusual step was taken to allow them to make revised bid and although the Fife company's management and employees took advantage of this, the announcement made on 10 June reconfirmed that Stagecoach was still the frontrunner in the bid to gain control of the company and remained the preferred bidder. This of course precluded

The minibuses and single deckers/coaches comprise Renault/Dodge S56s, MCW Metroriders, Leyland Leopards, Nationals and Tigers whilst the double deckers are, with four exceptions, Ailsa Volvos and Volvo B10MDs, and would thus bring Ailsas back into the Stagecoach combined fleet after a period of absence. Although the livery of the Fife fleet is cream & red, this would of course eventually give way to Stagecoach's corporate colour scheme, thus allowing the easier transfer of vehicles to and from other Group companies as and when necessary. Meanwhile, the fleet reorganisation was still continuing at Bluebird Northern, a number of whose Leyland Olympians were being despatched to Ribble Motor Services, their place being taken by a quantity of ex.Hastings Mercedes L608D minibuses transferred from Southdown and two more Bristol VRTs from Stagecoach Scotland Ltd.

One of a number of Duple coach-bodied Leyland Leopards operated in the fleet of Fife Scottish, 223 looks immaculate as it stands in the yard of Glenrothes depot in the spring of 1990. (K.A.Jenkinson)

Left : One of a large number of Alexander-bodied Ailsa Volvo double deckers operated by Fife Scottish, 832 (LSX32P) dates from 1975 and is seen here at Glenrothes depot.   (K.A.Jenkinson)

Below : Leaving Glenrothes bus station on a journey to Balfarg is Fife Scottish 7 (D879DSF), an Alexander-bodied 25-seat Dodge S56 painted in Buzzbus livery.   (K.A.Jenkinson)

Stagecoach from purchasing any further members of the Scottish Bus Group still to be privatised, as under the original ruling, no company was eligible to acquire more than two of the SBG's subsidiaries.

Should this deal be completed as is hopefully expected, the acquisition of Fife Scottish would give Stagecoach control of most of eastern Scotland from John o'Groats to the north bank of the Forth, with Grampian Transport, Strathtay Scottish and Tayside Transport being the only major operators sandwiched in this geographical area. Fife, who had in 1989 made a profit of £0.8million on a turnover of £14.9million serve the whole of Fife from depots at Aberhill, Cowdenbeath, Dunfermline, Glenrothes, Kirkcaldy, Newburgh and St.Andrews and operate a fleet of 300 vehicles comprising 53 minibuses, 93 single deckers, 88 double deckers and 66 coaches/dual purpose single deckers.

East Midland's coach-seated ECW-bodied Leyland Olympian 326 in corporate livery with Midland Travel fleet names leaves Mansfield bus station enroute to Worksop on 3 June 1991. (K.A.Jenkinson)

Looking to the future, following the lead taken by Stagecoach Malawi where an Employee Share Ownership Plan has been set up to purchase 15% of the Malawian Government's minority shareholding in the company for the benefit of the local workforce, Stagecoach Holdings are now planning to introduce an ESOP scheme for its UK employees. This will consist of two trusts - a 'Warehouse Trust' and a 'Profit Sharing Trust'. The Warehouse Trust is the vehicle to purchase all the shares which will be eventually owned by UK employees and initially it will borrow money to acquire around 10% of the ordinary shares of Stagecoach Holdings Ltd. from three sources. These are the 5% of the company's shares acquired by one of the company's previous bankers in July 1987; an issue of new shares earmarked for employees which was accepted by the company's institutional shareholders at the time of a successful private placing in December 1988 and a small percentage of existing shares held by Ann Gloag and Brian Souter since 1986.

The Warehouse Trust will then offer some of these shares to employees for cash while the remaining shares will be held until they are bought for employees by the Profit Sharing Trust. The Warehouse Trust will also buy back shares from employees who leave the Group or wish to divest themselves. From 1992, each year that the Group makes sufficient profit, a portion will be given to the Profit Sharing Trust who will use this to buy shares for employees from the Warehouse Trust and the general aim is to have the ESOP in place by the time of the company's AGM in October 1991.

Above : Passing through Eccles in November 1990 carrying the new-style Ribble fleet name and Stagecoach Holdings logo, is 1662 (JDB122N) an NCME-bodied Leyland Atlantean which was new to Greater Mancheter PTE and later operated in the fleet of Frontrunner South East.   (K.A.Jenkinson)

Following the gradual withdrawal of Stagecoach's Bristol Lodekkas, Bristol VRTs now form the backbone of the Perth double deck fleet. 091 (OTD151R) was one of several transferred from East Midland during 1990 and is seen here at Inveralmond depot in April 1991.   (K.A.Jenkinson)

A scene in the workshops at Stagecoach's Spittalfield depot on 26 April 1991 shows former East Midland Bristol VRT 116 (VTV167S) and recently-transferred ex.Bluebird Northern ECW--bodied Olympian 012 (TSO12X) receiving mechanical attention.   (K.A.Jenkinson)

The solid areas on this map show the operating territory of the Stagecoach Holdings subsidiaries throughout Britain while the striped area indicates the region covered by Fife Scottish which hopefully will have become part of the Stagecoach empire by the time this is read.

As far as Stagecoach are concerned, buses mean business, and since the company's entry into the field of passenger transport in 1980, its development and growth has been dramatic. Its successful 'hands-on' style of management, where the only place for passengers is on the buses, has extended the Group's activities across four continents and built up a fleet of almost 3,000 vehicles, all of which are gradually being transformed into a unified colour scheme to reflect Stagecoach's importance at home and overseas. Happily, the company has never lost sight of its past, brief as this may be, and within its subsidiary fleets has continued the preservation of several buses and coaches of yesteryear, adding to these when appropriate. As if to highlight the company's appreciation of vehicles of the past, although not part of the Stagecoach fleet, a former Glasgow Corporation B.U.T. single deck trolleybus has taken up temporary residency at the company's Spittalfield depot where it is currently being stored for its preservationist owners.

Although a period of consolidation has now been entered following the acquisition of its second former Scottish Bus Group member, a watchful eye is undoubtedly being kept on the transport industry both in Britain and overseas and should the opportunity be presented for further profitable expansion, no doubt this will be taken in true Stagecoach fashion. In any event, it would appear that a third volume will be necessary before the end of the century to further record the progress and development of the Stagecoach Group whose activities will undoubtedly continue to be a source of appeal to all who have an interest in road passenger transport.

Perhaps appropriately this book should end on a nostalgic note with a photograph of one of the vehicles with which Stagecoach began its operations. Purchased in September 1980, former Royal Blue ECW-bodied Bristol MW6G HDV639E originally carried the livery of GT Coaches, the company from which Stagecoach was born. Still owned and now regarded as part of the company's small fleet of preserved buses, HDV639E is seen here at Spittalfield in 1988 after receiving full Stagecoach livery.   (K.A.Jenkinson)